TORTOISESHELL

TORTOISESHELL

Maggie Campbell Pedersen

NAG
PRESS

First published in 2021 by NAG Press,
an imprint of The Crowood Press Ltd,
Ramsbury, Marlborough
Wiltshire SN8 2HR

enquiries@crowood.com

www.crowood.com

British Library Cataloguing-in-Publication Data
A catalogue record for this book is available from the British Library.

ISBN 978 0 7198 3144 7

Photo credits
All photos by the author, © Maggie Campbell Pedersen, unless otherwise stated.
All illustrated items are in private collections unless otherwise stated.

Typeset by Chapter One Book Production, Knebworth, UK

Printed in India by Parksons Graphics Pvt. Ltd., Mumbai.

Contents

Foreword

From the moment my curiosity for gems and gemmology started, back in the 1980s, I always had a thing for those gem materials that were produced by living organisms, the then so-called organic gems (now also known as biogenic gems). It was in the capacity of an avid gem knowledge addict that I met Maggie Campbell Pedersen, the author of numerous articles on that subject at *Gems & Jewellery* magazine, published by Gem-A (The Gemmological Association of Great Britain). Her vast knowledge was made into a book in 2004, *Gem and Ornamental Materials of Organic Origin*, which I still use as a reliable source of information on organic gem materials and their imitations. I met Maggie back in 2008 and got to know her better after I was elected vice-president of the Coral Commission of CIBJO, The World Jewellery Confederation, as we shared a common passion for gemmology and education; we soon started sharing information on coral and other gem materials.

Being from Portugal, where ivory art was quite important in the sixteenth and seventeenth centuries, I found her 2015 book *Ivory* a tremendous aid for a better understanding of the material and the imitations, especially the post late-1800s ones. Due to the same curiosity for art history with strong cultural heritage I was very happy when she told me she was preparing a new book, this time on tortoiseshell: a gem material that has been rather neglected in the gemmological literature. A few months later, I received a lovely email from her challenging me to write the foreword to this brand new title, a challenge that I accepted with great joy as Maggie is, if I may say so affectionately, the 'Organics Queen'.

The gem, jewellery and antiques' ecosystem is greatly enriched with the release of this comprehensive educational book. Tortoiseshell – actually a misnomer – is derived from the marine turtle, now a protected species that faces serious conservation challenges and is currently protected under global conservation regulations. However, it was extensively used in the past and up to now there has been no major resource of information on this organic gem for gemmologists, museum curators, antique dealers or art historians. The author, also known for her photography skills, had included a chapter in her 2004 book dedicated to the natural polymer produced by a few marine turtles, most notably the hawksbill turtle, that is known as tortoiseshell. But apart from that, Maggie's regular contributions to the *Gems & Jewellery* magazine, and the very few pages dedicated to this material in the traditional gemmological literature or in most gemmology course notes, it becomes clear that there is a need for a comprehensive and well-structured document on tortoiseshell. After many years of research, the author has added this book to the gemmological literature; it is an interesting and complete overview covering biology, history, nomenclature, biodiversity, conservation, treatments, imitations and, of course, gem identification.

As a gemmologist, I particularly enjoyed the chapters on identification, not only on the gemmological side with the explanations given on the classical gemmological techniques and the more complex and advanced laboratory methods, but also the distinguishing visual features that one should look for on an artefact to positively identify true tortoiseshell and separate it from the many lookalikes, such as horn, baleen and artificial products. The author cleverly organizes the section on artificial products in a chronological fashion, introducing the early imitations like celluloid from the late 1800s, as well as the early twentieth-century casein, and the modern plastics like acrylic, polyester or PVC.

One of the most interesting facts that we learn from this book is that tortoiseshell is a natural polymer, and therefore a 'natural plastic' – a term that is usually associated with artificial imitations of gems that are in fact better described as synthetic or semi-synthetic plastics. We should be much more careful when using the word 'plastic' in gemmology, as the term has a complex meaning.

The numerous applications of tortoiseshell, besides jewellery, receive good attention here. Many uses of the material are known in the decorative arts, namely in marquetry such as Boulle style, in Japanese Bekko work, in piqué work and in moulding scutes together as in Indo-Portuguese sixteenth/seventeenth-century small caskets. The use of this gem in ancient times is also discussed, although there are very few examples of the material in archaeological sites due to its lack of durability. The challenges in the manufacturing techniques of tortoiseshell also receive attention in this book, which is valuable information for those involved in the conservation of artefacts.

To conclude, this book is not only a great source to a gemmologist for the identification of tortoiseshell and its most common imitations, but also a relevant reference for decorative art historians, antique dealers, art conservators and collectors as an aid to the understanding of this extraordinary natural plastic produced by marine turtles.

Rui Galopim de Carvalho FGA DGA
Vice-President CIBJO, Section A
Founder, Portugal Gemas Academy

Dedication

For my sister Alison, and in memory of my brother Neil.
With my love.

Introduction

To see a hawksbill turtle emerge slowly from the sea is like witnessing something from a pre-historic world. To watch as she then drags her heavy body up the beach to a suitable spot to make a nest, proceeds to work at digging the nest, laying the eggs and then covering them and disguising the nest, fills one with awe. An hour and a half later, and surely exhausted, she drags herself back to the sea, leaving the eggs to incubate and then her babies to hatch about sixty days later. Just as awe-inspiring is to see the babies emerge from the nest and scramble down the beach as fast as their little flippers will carry them, and then see them tossed about in the waves at the water's edge before they determinedly swim out to sea, apparently none the worse for the experience. Knowing the perils that await them in the sea is heartbreaking and one cannot be surprised that so few make it to adulthood.

Twenty years ago I spent two weeks patrolling beaches in Barbados at night, watching the nesting process, checking the nests, marking them, measuring and tagging turtles, and collecting hatchlings from hotel lobbies, the lights of which they had mistaken for the horizon. Sometimes I sat in the sand watching a nesting turtle inadvertently dig up another nest, the eggs flying out behind her as she swept the sand with her back flippers. Turtle eggs are not easy to catch, especially in the dark. We reburied them, but their chances of survival were minimal. At other times we had to dig up the whole nest and choose a better location for the eggs because the turtles did not always choose wisely.

Turtles are slow and they look ancient. They are not warm and cuddly. They show no emotions. Yet they are utterly fascinating. So too is the horny material that covers the shells of some of them, called tortoiseshell. It is very beautiful when worked, and the craftsmanship and skill required has to be admired.

In no way would I wish to harvest tortoiseshell from turtles today; however, in order to protect the animals it is necessary to know about them. In order to follow the various laws on trade in endangered species we need to recognize tortoiseshell when we come across it. Furthermore, tortoiseshell is very beautiful, it has a long history and it features in some exquisite items in the world of decorative arts.

Tortoiseshell has been admired and used for decorative purposes for thousands of years. Because of the nature of the material there are no very old examples still in existence – the oldest is unlikely to be more than 400 to 500 years old. It is, therefore, difficult to say with certainty exactly where and how it was used, so that must be deduced from early writings. Even then, it is not always clear, as the material might, for example, be mentioned in a list of trade goods, but with no mention made of the use to which it was put. Further, 'turtle shell' might refer to a whole carapace and not just the scutes, and often no differentiation was made between tortoises and turtles, or between marine turtles and freshwater turtles living in lakes and rivers. It is only when the description is more specific that it is possible to deduce that the material is the scutes of marine turtles; that is, what we today call tortoiseshell.

Turtles and tortoises have been the subject of myths and legends for many millennia, and have been regarded as symbols of steadfastness, longevity and even immortality. Their images can be found depicted in cultures wherever the animals might have been encountered, from Ancient Egyptian tomb paintings and Assyrian carvings, to Ancient Mayan art and Australian Aboriginal cave paintings. The animals have been connected with ceremonies and rituals, and in some places are considered to be divine. In Burma, tortoises were kept in the grounds of sacred pagodas and fed delicacies, while the second incarnation of the Hindu deity, Vishnu, is said to have been as a turtle. In many cultures it was believed that a turtle held the world on its back. In North America, the Mohawk tribe believed that earthquakes were caused by the turtle stretching. Some myths told that the world was held up by four elephants, and they, in turn, stood on the back of a turtle. The creator goddess, Nuwa, in Chinese folklore used the legs of a turtle to prop up the sky after the water god GongGong destroyed the mountain upon which it had been resting. In Greek mythology, Apollo turned into a turtle to woo Dryope, the daughter of Dryops, King of Eurytus, and Aphrodite was depicted with a turtle as a symbol of fertility. Turtles have been depicted on coinage and stamps. They have also been popular in heraldry. When you start looking, turtles are everywhere.

The confusion regarding turtles or tortoises lasts to this day, as in some countries – for example, the USA – all the species may be called turtles. In others, including the UK, 'turtles' refers to those that live mainly or partly in water, while tortoises are their land-based cousins. In this book, the UK version is used.

The title of the book could be regarded as a misnomer too, because tortoiseshell is not the shell of tortoises but comes from marine turtles. The use of the word tortoiseshell may have arisen because early English naturalists called turtles 'sea tortoises'. It would, therefore, follow that their shells would be tortoise-shell.

Tortoiseshell has been used for a multitude of different things, and in many parts of the world. Mostly it has been used for adornment. The most common items made through the ages are combs, but boxes of some sort probably come a close second.

Today tortoiseshell is still part of our lives. Imitation tortoiseshell spectacle frames, combs and hair slides are everyday items. 'Tortoiseshell' is as popular as it has ever been. And turtles should be protected because it should not be forgotten that a turtle holds up the world.

Maggie Campbell Pedersen, April 2020

Acknowledgements

Only when putting pen to paper – or fingers to keyboard – do you realize just how little you know about a subject. So you start reading, and that results in a lot of questions. So you start asking, which also results in more questions, because every answer makes you more curious and wanting even more information.

As always, I have been amazed at how willing people have been to help and to share their knowledge. I have had meetings with museum conservators and curators, and I have contacted complete strangers by email. Never once was I turned away. I have also been met with immense patience; indeed, one or two people must, in the end, have logged on to their computers each day with fingers crossed that there wasn't another email from me awaiting their attention.

The people to whom I owe thanks are too numerous to mention here. Some have helped with a single piece of information, some with an introduction to someone else, and some have given me many hours and a lot of advice. My gratitude is sincere to each and every one. I could not have written this without that help.

There are a few people who must be mentioned by name: Dr George Hughes of Cape Town, leading expert on marine turtles and their conservation, helped me to keep on track with information about turtles; Ulli Freyer, furniture restorer in Bern, Switzerland, spent a whole day talking with me about tortoiseshell; Stéphane Ciccione, Director at Kélonia Sea Turtle Observatory, Réunion, answered questions about farmed turtles; Dr Caroline Solazzo at the Smithsonian, Washington, introduced me to proteomics; and Prof. Julia Horrocks, University of the West Indies, Barbados, introduced me to hawksbill turtles at the Barbados Sea Turtle Project twenty years ago.

Thanks also go to Prof. Tom Higham, Oxford Radiocarbon Accelerator Unit; Ayako Naito, Chief Liaison Officer Gem-A, Japan; Michael Hügi, Director Swiss Gemmological Society; William Wold, Chairman Vereniging Gemma; Dr Tony Tucker, Dr Scott Whiting and Dr Bob Prince of the Marine Science Program, Department of Parks and Wildlife, Western Australia; Alexis Kugel, Galerie J. Kugel, Paris; Rui Galopim de Carvalho, Vice-President Sector A, CIBJO; Patrick Daly, Senior Gemmology Tutor at Gem-A; and my fellow gemmologists at Gem-A, the Gemmological Association of Great Britain.

At the museums, I am greatly indebted to the following: Iskander Breebart, conservator at the Rijksmuseum in Amsterdam, and Jan Dorscheild, also at the Rijksmuseum; Thijs Boers, curator at The Amsterdam Museum; Kolokesa Mahina-Tuai, Fuli Pereira and Sabine Weik at the Auckland War Memorial Museum; Rebecca Fisher and Yvonne Carrillo-Huffman at the Australian Museum in Sydney, and many people at The Victoria and Albert Museum in London, especially Joanna Whalley, Senior Metalwork Conservator.

There are always some mistakes in a book and I take this opportunity to apologize for them. They are entirely my fault.

Finally, I would like to thank my friends and my family for their patience with me while I have been engrossed in turtle and tortoiseshell research, especially my daughters Louise and Kathrine, who are not only patient but also never cease to be encouraging.

Maggie Campbell Pedersen, April 2020

Chapter 1

Turtle Species

Introduction

Marine turtles are reptiles. They belong to the order Testudines, which also includes tortoises and terrapins, though marine turtles are often referred to as chelonians, as they belong to the family Cheloniidae. Strictly speaking, turtles live almost entirely in the sea, terrapins live in fresh water, such as ponds or rivers, and often bask on land, and tortoises live entirely on land.

In some countries, all three types of reptile are called turtles, and in others, including England, 'turtles' refers to those that live mainly or partly in water, while tortoises are their land-based cousins.

Turtles differ from tortoises in several ways, the most obvious being that they are not terrestrial. In order to move on land, tortoises have legs and feet, rather than flippers for swimming, and they have developed the ability to withdraw their extremities into their hard shells for protection. It is likely that attempts have been made to use the scutes from all the hard-shelled turtles and tortoises as tortoiseshell, but, with the possible exception of the radiated tortoise's beautiful shell from Madagascar, there are no records of this being successful with anything other than some

Fig. 1.
Paper-thin scutes from a tortoise.

Fig. 2.
Sturdy scutes from a hawksbill turtle.

Fig. 3.
Young green turtle (*Chelonia mydas*) near Barbados.

marine turtles. The keratinous covering on the shells of tortoises is generally very thin and would have little practical use to anything but the tortoise, where it acts as a protective layer (Figs. 1 and 2).

Marine turtles are found world-wide in tropical and sub-tropical waters. They live and forage in one area and migrate to another to mate and nest. After their nesting season, they return to their favourite foraging grounds. They repeat the migration throughout their lives, covering many thousands of kilometres in the process (Fig.3). Reptiles are often referred to as being cold-blooded animals, yet they have to maintain a certain temperature. Many animals, such as fish, marine mammals and marine turtles, are ectotherms. This means that they regulate their internal body temperature by responding to changes in the temperature around them. Turtles need the warmth of the water to function. If they get too cold, they slow down and eventually die, which is probably the reason why they can sometimes be seen basking in the sun. Research undertaken in the Persian Gulf has shown hawksbills that forage in the shallow waters there apparently get too hot in mid-summer when the surface temperature of the water can rise a few degrees, so they migrate to deeper water. After a month or two, when the temperatures drop again, they return to their favourite area in shallower waters. Only leatherback turtles are able to regulate their body temperatures to maintain a constant 30°C, so they can occasionally be seen foraging near ice floes.

Origin and Species

The origin of marine turtles is not totally clear. It is still being debated whether they are descended from the same animals as birds and crocodiles, or whether they descend from a form of lizard.

From fossil remains, it is reckoned that a proto turtle, which had a partial shell, existed about 250 million years ago. It is known that later turtles could grow to an immense size. The remains of one found in a coal mine in Colombia has been named *Carbonemys cofrinii*, meaning 'coal turtle'. It was large enough to eat small crocodiles and had a shell that measured 172cm. Its estimated age is 60 million years. Older and bigger was *Archelon ischyros*, the largest marine turtle ever discovered. Found in South Dakota, USA, it was 4m long but is not thought to have had a shell and so resembled more today's leatherback turtle.

Over millions of years, marine turtles have reduced in size but otherwise have not changed very much. The various families have split into different species but the majority are now extinct, so that today there are only seven extant species.

The leatherback turtle is the largest and is in a family of its own: Dermochelyidae, genus *Dermochelys coriacea*. It can grow to over 2m in length. Leatherbacks have no shell but a tough, leathery skin containing bony plaques.

The remaining six marine turtles all have hard shells and all belong to the family Cheloniidae. They are sometimes referred to as chelonians. Three of them have not been used for tortoiseshell: the little Kemps ridley turtle (*Lepidochelys kempii*); the olive ridley

Fig. 4.
Loggerhead turtle
(*Caretta caretta*).
GEORGE HUGHES

turtle (*Lepidochelys olivacea*), which is also small; and the flatback turtle (*Natator depressus*), which lives only around Australia.

The horny plates (called scutes) on the shells of the remaining three can be used as tortoiseshell. They are: first and foremost, the hawksbill turtle (*Eretmochelys imbricata*), which is famous for the quality of its tortoiseshell and has been the most used; the green turtle (*Chelonia mydas*), which has also been used for tortoiseshell but which is possibly more famous as a source of meat and the basis of turtle soup, and is called 'green' because it has a fat layer that is slightly green in colour; and the loggerhead turtle (*Caretta caretta*), the tortoiseshell from which was used only occasionally (Fig. 4).

Hawksbill Turtles (*Eretmochelys imbricata*)

Hawksbill turtles are found around the globe, though they stay almost exclusively in warm, tropical waters. They are the smallest and least abundant of the three species. Their size varies but, on average, they grow to about 90cm carapace length, weigh about 75kg and reach maturity at twenty-five to thirty years.

Hawksbills have scutes that can grow to almost 1cm in thickness and have a random mottled pattern (Fig. 5).

The main breeding and nesting grounds for hawksbills are around the Caribbean and Costa Rica, the east coast of Africa, Madagascar, Saudi Arabia, the north-east coast of Australia around the Great Barrier Reef, and Indonesia, the Philippines and Papua New Guinea. They also nest in many other places, including the southernmost part of Japan.

As their favourite diet is sponges, they live and forage around coral reefs, where they keep the invasive species down, allowing the corals to flourish. The turtles can eat up to eight times their body weight in sponges per annum. Favourite foraging grounds are off the coasts of Panama, Nicaragua, the Bahamas, and the islands of Micronesia and Melanesia. Some turtles stay near their nesting grounds, but most migrate anything between 60 and 300km or more to their foraging areas.

Fig. 5. ►
Section of an unpolished hawksbill turtle scute, seen by transmitted light, causing the growth rings to show through.

Green Turtles (*Chelonia mydas*)

Greens are the largest of the three species and also the most numerous of all marine turtles. Again, their size varies but, on average, an adult reaches about 130cm and can weigh more than 210kg. It has been noted that captive-bred green turtles grow and mature much faster than those in the wild due to their artificial diet of specially prepared, nutrient-rich pellets, and can reach sexual maturity as early as five years old (Fig. 6).

Green turtles are found in both tropical and sub-tropical waters. They nest in most of the same places as hawksbills, and in many more besides; for example, in Florida, Ascension Island, the Seychelles and the eastern end of the Mediterranean. There are very large nesting populations in Oman and the south-western Indian Ocean, especially on the scattered islands around Madagascar. There are also many in the Great Barrier Reef of Australia.

The mottled pattern of a green's carapace is more defined than that of a hawksbill and often has a radiating pattern, but the scutes are thin.

The East Pacific green turtle is found along the coasts from Baja California to Chile. It has darker colouring on both its carapace and plastron, is slightly smaller and is sometimes called a 'black turtle'.

Fig. 6.
Young green turtle.

There have been discussions about whether it should be classified as a different species or sub-species.

Greens are mostly herbivorous as adults, preferring to forage off-shore in shallower waters than hawksbills or loggerheads in order to find the sea grasses that comprise the bulk of their diet, though they also eat some algae and small animal prey, such as jellyfish. They tend to migrate between 200 and 800km to their feeding grounds, with a maximum distance recorded on a tagged turtle of 2,850km.

Loggerhead Turtles (*Caretta caretta*)

Loggerhead turtles can be almost as large as greens, with a maximum weight of about 200kg and a length of up to 110cm. Their average age at sexual maturity is reckoned to be about thirty-five years. Loggerhead nesting grounds are more widespread than those of hawksbills and greens. They nest in some of the same places as the other two species, but also further south on Africa's east coast, on Australia's west coast and as far north as Japan. They are the most prevalent marine turtle in the Mediterranean, but it is Florida that has the most nesting loggerheads. There is also a big nesting colony on Oman's Masirah Island.

Loggerheads have thin scutes, like those of the greens, and have heavier pigmentation, giving a darker colouring with less distinct mottling on their carapaces.

Of the three species, loggerheads tend, on average, to migrate the furthest to their feeding grounds. Many choose the Atlantic Ocean from Brazil to Canada, concentrating on the area around the Bahamas and Mexico. They are also found in the seas around southern Africa and Madagascar, the Arabian Peninsula, and further to the Far East and Australia. Tagged turtles have been measured feeding 200–600km from their breeding areas, with a maximum distance measured of about 3,500km.

Hybrids

It is known that cross-breeding occurs between some turtles and that there are examples of hawksbill and loggerhead hybrids, especially around the coast of Brazil where their nesting activities overlap. Research is ongoing to learn more about them. Of the examples seen so far, they appear to pick up characteristics from both species; for example, the serrated edge of the carapace of the hawksbill and the larger head of the loggerhead. The quality and colour of their scutes has not yet been noted.

Turtle Anatomy and Life Cycle

Precisely how the turtle's shell developed has puzzled scientists for centuries. It is an odd construction that, apparently, has not changed greatly for many millennia. The anatomy of the three turtles is very similar. They have a dorsal (back) shell called a carapace and a ventral (belly) shell called a plastron. Over the bony skeleton of both carapace and plastron is a layer of horny plates called scutes, beneath which is the dermis from which they grow. The horny material is keratin, which is an insoluble protein akin to nails, hair, beaks and claws (*see* Chapter 3). The bones of the spine and ribs are joined to the carapace and edged by a row of small bones called peripheral bones (Fig. 7). The bones in the plastron consist mainly of shoulder and abdominal bones.

The keratinous scutes on the plastron are pale in colour and vary in number with each species, also sometimes varying within the species too. Those on the carapace are darker and mottled. The mottled carapace of a hawksbill has five central scutes, four on each side of the shell and twelve small ones on each side around the edge called marginals. The marginals give the outline of the hawksbill's carapace a slightly serrated look (Fig. 8).

A newly hatched turtle's body is soft and its shell is flexible, to enable it to lie curled up inside the egg. As turtles mature, their shells become harder and more ossified, the ribs grow in length to meet the peripheral bones, and the gaps between the ribs, called fontanelles, become smaller as the ribs increase in size and develop a layer of bone in between. In fully mature loggerheads, the fontanelles are replaced entirely by bone, but adult hawksbills

Fig. 7. Skeleton of a hawksbill turtle (*Eretmochelys imbricata*). PHOTO BY KIND PERMISSION OF THE NATIONAL MUSEUM OF NATURAL HISTORY, SMITHSONIAN INSTITUTION

and greens retain the fontanelles at the outer edge and towards the back of the body, instead filling the gaps with cartilage (Fig. 9). Research has suggested that greens actually lose some of the bone and replace it with cartilage as they age, in order to lighten their load and make long-distance swimming easier. Loggerheads, on the other hand, dive to greater depths and must withstand more pressure, so the extra weight would be an advantage.

The cartilage between the bones in the plastron is called calipee, and that between the ribs in the carapace is called calipash. It is these sheets of cartilage that were cut out, dried and reconstituted to make turtle soup (*see* Chapter 7).

The turtle's head and flippers have scales of keratin, though this

Fig. 8. Polished carapace of a hawksbill turtle. ALAN HODGKINSON

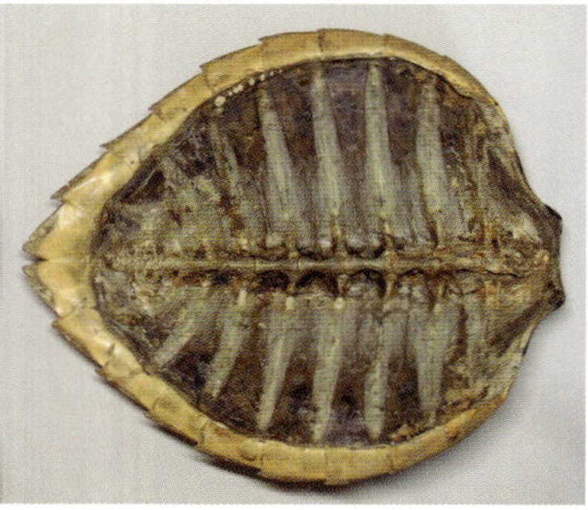

Fig. 9. Underside of the carapace of a hawksbill turtle. ALAN HODGKINSON

is not as hard as the scutes on its shell. The number of head scales and carapacial scutes are species-specific, enabling identification. The skin on the neck and sides of the turtle is moderately keratinized but without scales. The skin, together with the flippers, has been used as leather. Unlike many reptiles, turtles do not slough off their skin.

The three species of turtle have different shaped beaks to deal with their different diets. This can also help in identification. The hawksbill eats mainly sponges and has a slightly pointed beak with which to bite off pieces of sponge in the coral reefs (Fig. 10). The beak resembles, slightly, that of a hawk, hence the turtle's name. Loggerheads live on crustaceans and have strong, pointed beaks with which to crunch their prey, but the points get worn down as the turtle ages. Greens have much blunter looking beaks with serrated edges for tearing at the sea grass on which they feed.

Turtles are designed to be light and streamlined in water in order to be energy efficient and have good buoyancy. In water they can move fast, using the front flippers to do the swimming and the rear ones as rudders. On land, their bodies are cumbersome and they move slowly, pushing themselves forward across the sand on their bellies.

All three can hold their breath for a long time underwater, depending upon their level of activity. A resting or sleeping turtle can remain underwater for several hours but eventually it must come to the surface to breathe, though loggerheads and green turtles have been recorded as hibernating under water for some months. During normal activity turtles surface every 45 to 60min.

Their dives can take them to significant depths in search of their food. Loggerhead dives have been measured to a depth of 600m, but greens and hawksbills do not dive nearly as deep, reaching about 110 and 100m, respectively. During a deep dive, the plastron becomes concave due to the water pressure, which is possible because a turtle has fewer rigid bones on the ventral side of its body.

A fully grown turtle's size depends largely on where it spends

Fig. 10.
Hawksbill turtle, showing the 'hawk's beak'.
GEORGE HUGHES

most of its time, and within the same species can differ by 20cm or more according to its location, diet and the temperature of the water.

Turtles live almost their entire lives in water. It is extremely rare for a male ever to venture ashore again once it has reached the sea after hatching, though there are occasional sightings of both males and females basking in the sun in a quiet, unpopulated area. The females, on the other hand, have to come ashore to lay their eggs. Having done so, they do not incubate the eggs but return to the sea and have nothing more to do with their offspring. In between nesting seasons they swim off to their foraging grounds, which may be nearby but can also be thousands of kilometres away, not returning till the next time they mate and nest, usually two to three years later.

One of the questions that puzzle biologists and conservationists is why would a turtle, for example, a hawksbill, that has nested near the Great Barrier Reef where sponges are plentiful, travel to some island hundreds of kilometres away to forage? This urge to swim great distances between nesting and foraging grounds affects all three species. Furthermore, after nesting, individual turtles go off on their own and don't necessarily swim in the same direction as other turtles. Occasionally, it is noted that a turtle doesn't go far; for example, a hawksbill that was tagged as an adolescent in Hawaii was picked up a few times in the same location over a period of twenty years, and then seen nesting on a nearby beach.

There have been sightings recorded of a hawksbill exhibiting bioluminescence – the whole turtle glowing a green colour. It is extremely rare and, as yet, the cause is unknown, though there is speculation that it could be because the turtles have consumed corals known to be bioluminescent.

Some species of marine turtle come ashore in large groups to nest, but the hawksbill, green and loggerhead are all solitary nesters. Most turtles mate and nest near the beach where they emerged as hatchlings, sometimes even on the same beach. If a female nests far away, it is probably because she has become lost on her return journey. That they migrate was first presumed a long time ago, though originally without proof. It was not known where they went, but it was surmised that it was associated with the major ocean currents. In recent years, mitochondrial DNA (mtDNA) has

Fig. 11.
Female hawksbill turtle returning to the sea after nesting.

been used because it can prove the relationship between hatchlings and nesting turtles, and connects them to turtles at feeding grounds far away. It does not, however, track the animals.

Nesting females can sometimes look as though they are crying, but the 'tears' are not from the eyes. They come from a gland very close to the eye, which produces very salty mucus. Consuming as much salt as a turtle does, living in salt-water, would be detrimental to the animal if it was not able to expel it via the gland. Turtle emotions are as yet not understood, as there is little recognizable display.

A female turtle may mate with several males, and she can store the sperm until it suits her to lay her eggs. Nesting is a laborious process, as the female must first haul herself ashore and well up the beach, dig a body pit for herself to lie in, and then a gourd-shaped hole nearly a metre deep for the egg chamber. Using her hind flippers, she scoops the sand out and tosses it aside till the chamber is the right size and shape. It is worth remembering that she cannot see what she is doing and the operation is carried out by instinct. Having deposited one hundred or more eggs into the hole, she then covers it again with her hind flippers, compacting the sand as she goes, and finally sweeps more sand around to camouflage the nest. The process takes at least an hour and often two. The eggs are round, white, about the size of table tennis balls and soft in order not to be damaged as they fall into the hole. The shells become slightly harder during incubation, but not rigid. They are porous, so allowing oxygen, which has penetrated through the grains of sand into the nest, to reach the embryos.

Provided that the nest is in a suitable place and is not raided by any other animals (*see* Chapter 2), the eggs remain and develop in the nest for approximately sixty days. The number of eggs laid is very large, but it is today estimated that only about one in a thousand will result in a mature turtle several years later.

After incubation, the hatchlings break out of their shells using the 'egg tooth', which is a little point on the top of their beaks that later disappears, and clamber to the surface of the sand. This takes about four days and, as a rule, they emerge at night when there

Fig. 12.
Hawksbill hatchlings making their way to the sea after hatching.

are fewer predators around, usually all emerging at more or less the same time, as there is safety in numbers. At this stage they weigh between 20 and 30g. Following the light on the horizon, they scramble as fast as they can to the sea (Fig. 12). This is a perilous journey as they are a favourite diet of crabs, as well as many other animals. Reaching the surf, they are tossed around but continue their swim, covering up to 20km in the next twenty or so hours. This is called the 'swim frenzy'. They carry the remainder of the egg yolk with them, which supplies enough food for up to two weeks. The hatchlings stop when they reach an area of driftwood or a sargassum raft where they can rest and float with the current. It is believed that they do this until they are big and strong enough to start swimming and diving for their food, until then subsisting on whatever drifts by. Hawksbills will find a reef to start foraging for sponges when they are two to three years old, but greens and loggerheads have been known to float around on ocean gyres for a decade.

This is the stage at which the turtles travel furthest. For a long time no-one knew where they went until they reappeared at breeding grounds, but it is now believed that they just keep floating or swimming, carried by the currents and the ocean gyres. This period is called 'the lost years'. Most turtles do not reach maturity; those that do possess a determination to return 'home', and if they are unfortunate enough to have been carried half-way round the world this determination will take them back to where they were hatched. Journeys made by them have been measured at many thousands of kilometres; for example, from Australia to Peru or, as hatchlings, from Japan to Mexico and back as sub-adults, or as adults a round trip via Australia – distances of tens of thousands of kilometres – in order to return to the area where they hatched and to start the whole process again (*see* Chapter 2). It is probably on this journey that they find their foraging grounds, to which they will later return after breeding.

The size of fully grown turtles of the same species can vary substantially from region to region, as can the age at which they reach sexual maturity, which can be anything from seventeen to forty years. Their lifespan is also difficult to determine. Until a turtle reaches maturity it may be possible to judge its approximate age by its size, but after that it is impossible to judge by sight how old it is, and difficult even by testing. Various methods to determine age have been tried, for example: by examining the mottled pattern on the carapacial scutes, which is not very reliable; counting the growth rings in scutes, which is not reliable either as the layers are not laid down regularly and a turtle can periodically stop producing the keratin that forms the layers; using skeletochronology, in which the growth marks in cross-sections of the long bones in the flippers are counted; and by carbon 14 testing of layers in the turtle's keratin, because turtles absorb radiocarbon in their diet and it is laid down in the keratin. Of these, only the first can be carried out on a live turtle, and the last test is only feasible on hawksbill scutes, as only they are of sufficient thickness. All these test results can only give calculated ages and must be compared against equal tests carried out on a turtle of confirmed age to validate the estimations. However, it is reasonable to assume that marine turtles live at least forty to fifty years in the wild and, possibly, live considerably longer than that. There is a known example of a loggerhead returning to the same beach to nest for thirty-five years, and she probably reached sexual maturity at about thirty-five years, so would have been seventy years old when last seen.

Chapter 2

Conservation and the Dangers Faced by Turtles Today

Introduction

The first conservation legislation ever recorded concerned the harvesting of marine turtles. The 'Act agaynst the killinge of ouer young Tortoyses', was brought in 400 years ago in Bermuda, when it was realized that overfishing was depleting the stocks of the animals, described as '...so excellent a fishe...'. Taking any turtle measuring less that 18in (46cm) was prohibited. The fine for doing so was fifteen pounds of tobacco. Sadly, it was to be another 350 years before anything was done to protect turtles world-wide and, in the meantime, their numbers in the oceans were decimated.

Marine turtles are some of the world's most fascinating animals. They were around with the dinosaurs and outlived them. They are pre-historic relics, slow-moving and puzzling. Very little was known of the natural history of marine turtles until the 1930s, when a biologist by the name of Archie Carr began to study them and publish papers on the subject, and even now there are many questions still to be answered. In order to protect turtles, it is necessary to understand more about them.

For many years it has been feared that turtles are in danger of becoming extinct and that efforts must be made to protect them. Happily, it can now be seen that nesting turtle numbers are recovering in many parts of the world, thanks to diligent work by conservationists. But they are not out of danger yet.

Conservation is a relatively new phenomenon. For thousands of years it was not appreciated that resources needed to be conserved and that they were not unlimited. When at last the idea of animal conservation was mooted in the early twentieth century, it was only in regard to conserving resources and had nothing to do with the welfare of the animals. Further, it is worth remembering that when animals were cruelly treated in the past it was not with malicious intent, but because no-one knew any better. Animals were not regarded as sentient beings.

Conservation is expensive and it is not an exact science; indeed, it has been called an experimental science. It is conducted by trial and error, and as more vital knowledge of a species is gained, the methods used are refined to suit the species. Research and conservation go hand in hand because one method does not fit all, and the methods used for each species may have to be varied according to geographical conditions and local culture. It is very difficult to explain to local people who live a meagre existence on some far-flung island that they can no longer catch a turtle to feed their family because the turtle's life is perceived by some to be more important.

The Need to Learn More

Marine turtle conservation has its own specific complications. First, the turtles spend almost their entire lives at sea. When once they are hatched, they head straight for the sea, and from then on essentially only the females return to land to lay eggs. It was a long time before it was realized that an individual female can return to the same beach three, four or even more times in a season, so it was originally believed that there were many times the number of turtles arriving than was the case. On the other hand, turtles tend only to nest every two or three years, so that also warped the figures. These riddles began to be understood when turtles were tagged. The early methods of flipper tagging were not successful though, and few kept their tags on for long. Further, hatchlings weighing 25g could not wear a big tag, so little was known about what happened to them, where they went or their mortality rate when they hatched and swam out to sea. Tagging methods improved and today it is still a useful resource (Fig. 13).

Another problem with turtle conservation is that success is based mostly on the numbers of females that are nesting in any season at a given place. Compared with humans, female turtles do not mature until they are quite old; for instance, loggerheads mature at an average age of twenty-five years, so it is therefore impossible to tell in the short term what the effects of any conservation effort may be.

Little research has been done into how turtles use their brains and what might be termed their 'intelligence', but it is known that

Fig. 13.
Juvenile hawksbill turtle that has been caught whilst swimming, for measuring, weighing and tagging.

they have a small brain compared to their body size. Yet they have survived for over 100 million years, through the mass extinction that wiped out the dinosaurs and much else besides. It was not until humankind began to travel the world that turtles came under threat, and where 300–400 years ago there were plenty of turtles around the globe, today their numbers are hugely reduced. It is reckoned that there are only about 22,000 nesting female hawks-bills left, though that is only a rough estimate as it is impossible to count turtles accurately.

Another conundrum was how far do the turtles travel? Originally, it was presumed that they travel only a short distance and stay in or near the area where they were hatched. An early method of tagging (with a reward offered if the animal was found), gave the first proof that some turtles travel many hundreds of kilo-metres. Later, when small satellite transponders were attached to a few turtles and the animals were followed by satellite telemetry, the full extent of their journeys could be mapped.

The theory that turtles return to or near their natal beach to nest was first suggested in the 1960s, but it was hard to prove until mtDNA, which is passed down through the female line, was used. By testing both hatchlings and the nesting females in any given rookery, it was found that they were related and that it was related turtles that returned to the area to nest. The mtDNA for the nesting and hatchling turtles in other rookeries was different.

DNA has been helpful in marine turtle research as it can also give an impression of where the turtles go, both as hatchlings during the lost years while they grow into adulthood, and then, when they start their mature adult lives, where they migrate to and from for nesting and feeding. DNA cannot be used to track them, but it can identify relationships.

The turtles' travels were becoming clearer with satellite track-ing, but satellite transponders are costly and can fail, so only a limited number of turtles could be tracked. There has also been some discussion as to whether the tracking devices hinder the turtles and change their behaviour or even endanger them in some way. In the instances where the transmitter worked well, though, it proved that turtles could swim a very long way. Although perhaps not the norm, some turtles have been tracked swimming over 35,000km.

The lost years were a puzzle for a long time. Originally thought to be just one lost year, it was believed that the hatchlings didn't go far. Co-operation with researchers in various countries and a database of the turtles' DNA have been enlightening. Some loggerhead hatchlings have hatched in Australia or Japan on one side of the Pacific Ocean and travelled across it to Baja California. That had been thought impossible and the results probably coincidental, but the DNA of some young turtles caught in drift nets in mid-Atlantic has shown them to be of the same extended family as the hatchlings and the juveniles on the other side of the ocean. They probably took several years to make their journey, and would take several more to get back again to start their adult lives (*see also* Chapter 1).

Even if the turtles drift with the currents as hatchlings because they cannot swim against them, their later travels are not arbitrary and they evidently have a keen sense of direction, though this is not yet fully understood. It seems that the females may swim with the currents to distant areas to feed, but then they swim back again to nest on or very near the beach where they were born, remain in the area for the whole nesting season and then swim away to their feeding grounds again. They return two or three years later and the cycle repeats itself. DNA and tagging has confirmed this, and there are examples of turtles nesting around the coasts of Florida but foraging in the waters off the eastern coast of Spain in the Mediterranean. Many theories have been put forward regarding what guides them, such as water temperature, wind direction or ocean currents. It now seems fairly certain that they use lines of magnetic force as a guide, though quite how is still a bit of a mystery. It was recently discovered that many marine turtle species have magnetite particles somewhere in their bodies; for example, in their inner ear. As the name implies, magnetite is a mineral that is slightly magnetic, but even with built-in magnets, turtle navigation is an incredible phenomenon.

Quite apart from the obvious natural dangers, such as cyclones, turtles face innumerable hazards from the moment the eggs are laid. Turtle eggs are a popular feast of rats, foxes, dogs, pigs, coyotes, jaguars, honey badgers and any animal local to the area that can dig. Hatchlings are easy prey for anything with a mouth, beak or claw big enough to grab a flipper. A great many hatchlings are caught by crabs as they make their way to the sea. Once in the sea, they can fall prey to numerous other marine predators, and while on the surface of the water to birds. It is reckoned that less than one in a thousand eggs will result in an adult turtle. Once they reach adulthood they have few natural predators, thanks to their size and hard shell. Nonetheless, they have one big enemy: humankind.

Human Impact

The start of the exploitation of the turtle populations was in the seventeenth century when westerners started to colonize the world and to take turtles for food and for their keratinous scutes, wiping out entire populations (*see* Chapter 7). Until then, the harvesting of turtles for local consumption had not had any adverse effect on their numbers.

Progress for the human race has not meant progress for turtles. Quite apart from being deliberately caught for food or as decoration, there are a myriad of dangers that marine turtles now encounter, thanks to humans. One huge problem is that turtles are being caught as bycatch by fishing vessels. If a turtle is caught and cannot resurface to breathe, it drowns. Turtles are renowned for being able to hold their breath for several hours in some situations, but in stressed circumstances their time limit is only about 15min.

The accidental catching of turtles in trawl nets by fishing vessels is being combatted by turtle excluder devices (TEDs). Gill nets are being strung out lower in the water to allow turtles to swim over them, and various types of fishing net are strung out using buoys that contain solar-powered lights, which deter the turtles. It is encouraged in long-line fishing to use G-shaped hooks rather than the customary J-shaped ones, as fewer turtles are snagged on the former because the point turns slightly inwards. No method, though, is foolproof. Turtles get caught in all manner of nets, such as those put out for bather protection around a beach or in lines for pearl oysters or in nets used for dredging shipping channels.

Discarded fishing tackle is one of the big menaces in the seas and many turtles lose their lives by becoming entangled – as do other marine animals that need to surface to breathe, such as whales. The immense size of the problem caused by discarded tackle and plastics in the oceans is only just coming to light. Indeed, plastic in the seas is even more dangerous than getting caught as bycatch by fishing vessels. Turtles can get caught up in pieces of plastic as mundane as the loops around six-pack drinks' cans, which hampers their swimming ability. They also eat plastic because they have no idea what it is and mistake it for food. A clear plastic bag floating in the sea can look a lot like a jellyfish. Plastic on some beaches impedes nesting and can injure a turtle, and it is dangerous for hatchlings, which can get caught, disoriented or just slowed down on their dangerous journey to the sea.

Chemicals in the sea are another danger to marine life. Not only oil spills from shipping, but also the run-off from agricultural fertilizers and insecticides and sewage can all have an effect – they are considered as possible reasons that turtles are suffering from an illness that can kill, called fibrous papilloma. The disease causes tumours on the turtle, especially around the softer parts, such as around the eyes where it can blind them, or internally where it destroys internal organs.

Turtles can be injured or killed by contact with a vessel, be it a large container ship on the open seas or small pleasure craft nearer to the shore. Disrupting turtles in any of their habits or usual progress can have a hugely detrimental effect, in some cases causing them to get completely lost. Such disruption happens with ships at sea, and also happens to hatchlings with inappropriate lighting on or near nesting beaches. A neonatal turtle cannot work out what is the horizon and what is the local discotheque (Fig. 14).

Fig. 14.
Box full of hawksbill hatchlings that were collected from a hotel lobby. They were later released from a beach nearby.

Hawksbills are not, basically, pelagic so are not as at risk as other turtles from large ships. Statistics would suggest that fewer hawksbills than other turtles are caught as bycatch. On the other hand, the ones that are caught have been taken intentionally and illegally.

Males or Females?

A lot of the data collected are from female turtles, because they are the ones that conveniently come ashore and can be tagged or microchipped or have samples taken. So what of the male turtles? And what is the ratio of the two sexes? Counting those caught in the sea may not help to answer the question, because not until an adolescent reaches about 60cm in length is it possible to see what sex the creature is. At that stage, a small tail emerges from beneath the carapace of a male turtle. Based on various data, recent calculations give a very approximate world-wide estimate of three females to one male, though in some places it is thought that nests may produce 90 per cent females.

Turtles are among the animals the sex of whose young is not determined at fertilization, but about a third of the way through the approximately sixty-day incubation period of the eggs. Higher temperatures in the nest produce more females, while cooler temperatures produce more males. Even nests dug on a beach in the shade of a tall building, such as a hotel, can produce fewer females. The temperature in a nest is usually between 24 and 33°C; for most turtles, the pivotal point – that is the point at which an equal number of each sex would develop – is about 29°C.

The sex ratio in any given clutch is calculated by the temperature of the nest during incubation and the duration of incubation. Warmer temperatures result in both more females and in shorter incubations or, if it is too hot, a raised mortality rate of the hatchlings. Further, a short incubation period can result in small hatchlings with less chance of survival.

The problem of higher beach temperatures is exacerbated in tourist spots. The natural flora and forests around some beaches have been cleared in order to plant the exotic imported trees and flowers favoured by tourists. This leaves the beaches more open and the sand warmer. Raised ambient temperatures caused by climate change will also result in more female turtles.

Climate change is impacting marine turtles in many ways, especially in the nesting season.

Rising sea-levels result in nesting beaches being reduced in area and previously dry stretches becoming flooded. It is possible that turtles will adapt over time and, instead of returning to their natal area, will find new, drier areas in which to nest where the temperature is cooler, but this is one of the many unknowns.

The hawksbills face another challenge from climate change, which is the dying off of coral reefs in some areas where they go to forage and eat sponges. This is happening largely due to sea temperatures, pollution and the changing acidity of the oceans.

In other areas, the scarcity of hawksbills has allowed the sponges to take over some healthy reefs, swamping and killing the corals. Hawksbills have been regarded as the gardeners of the coral reefs and, as such, are an important part of the ecosystem of the oceans.

Human Help

In an effort to learn more, numerous methods of research and conservation have been tried by dedicated professionals – and often volunteers too – around the world. One of the important things to understand is where the turtles go. In the waters off Réunion they are using the simple method of divers and photo ID to identify individual turtles, to see how long they stay in the area. As with zebras and their stripes, or leopards and their spots, each turtle has a slightly different spacing and shape to the scales on the side of its head.

The patrolling of beaches at night is still immensely valuable as it gives the basic information of how many females are nesting, where the nests are, how many eggs are in the nests and their mortality rate, and when a turtle is seen nesting in a totally inappropriate place such as a drainage ditch, the chance to dig up the eggs when she has finished laying, and to dig a new, safer nest as close as possible to the original one and re-bury the eggs. This has to be done immediately after laying, as within hours an embryo attaches to the inside of the shell and moving it would be likely to dislodge and kill it.

At the costly end of conservation is satellite telemetry, which can involve burying mock eggs containing tracking devices in the nests or attaching tracking devices to the turtles. DNA testing of large numbers of turtles is also expensive but has given invaluable information. A very new system of tracking turtles and watching their behaviour is through the use of drones, which have become much less expensive and more advanced in recent years. The full potential for this method has yet to be explored.

While climate change is a problem that needs to be tackled

world-wide, there are many ways in which the turtles can be directly helped. In order to protect nests from predators, numerous methods have been tried, including sprinkling chilli powder around them, but care has to be taken not to hurt emerging hatchlings. A web of bamboo poles over the nest keeps predators out, but it also shows them the exact location of the nest. Ideas that are known to have some success include all the innovations mentioned, which are being used by the fishing industry. Dim lighting on and around beaches lessens the risk of disorienting the hatchlings. Marking the nest sites can prevent tourists from compacting the sand on the beaches, which hinder the hatchlings' emergence, even though it is an advertisement. Local people, especially the children, are being educated about the turtles' needs, as are tourists. Fortunately, the days when people thought it fun to ride on the back of a turtle to race it on the beach are now gone, and most tourists understand that turtles should neither be touched nor approached, and that indiscriminate use of bright lights, such as torches, can disorientate them.

The international agreement between governments called CITES (Convention on International Trade of Endangered Species of Flora and Fauna) covers international trade only and each country makes its own domestic laws (*see* Appendix I). Several countries originally joined CITES with a reservation about turtles, but slowly all members have dropped their reservations and banned any import or export of any turtle or part thereof, including tortoiseshell. Most countries have also banned domestic use, but not all.

Japan was one of the last countries to drop its reservation and is still producing work in tortoiseshell from its own hawksbill turtles, though on a far smaller scale than before when it was the world's largest importer of hawksbill scutes, accounting for 80 per cent of the world's trade.

In some places there is an abundance of turtles, and those countries would like to be permitted to export tortoiseshell legally to places like Japan where working tortoiseshell is regarded as a custom. Many people – including some conservationists and experts – believe that, properly managed, a turtle harvest is sustainable. An equal number are vehemently opposed to the idea. One of the arguments against, concerns to which country the turtles belong: the one where they nest or the one where they forage offshore? Without being able to answer that question, it is unlikely that legal trade will be resumed.

Poaching, on the other hand, is still rife and there are countries that still export, import and sell tortoiseshell items from illegally caught turtles (Fig. 15). Most of the illegal international trade in tortoiseshell starts with the fishing of hawksbills by small, artisanal fisheries, which sell to the international networks that are also trading in other illegal items, such as drugs or other endangered species.

Fig. 15.
Tortoiseshell and mother-of-pearl hair-slide, illegally sold in the Far East.

Human Intervention in the Breeding Programmes

Many years ago, there were efforts to re-introduce turtles to beaches where they no longer nested and, over a period of several years, thousands of hatchlings were collected and flown in small aircraft to secluded spots to be released. The practice was abandoned as there was no way of telling whether it was successful or not. In a later endeavour, thousands of eggs were collected and transported to different beaches in southern Africa. There was a 77 per cent hatching success, which was promising, but because of the length of time it takes for adults to return, the final outcome is unknown.

So-called head starting is another method that has been tried. It involves catching wild hatchlings and rearing them for nine to twelve months in large tanks for release when they are a lot bigger and, therefore, less vulnerable and less easy prey. The idea was controversial, as many thought that it stopped the hatchlings from imprinting in their brains where to find their natal beaches, and also the hatchlings would have no idea how to fend for themselves once they were released. No-one has the answer, and head starting is not much used today.

Turtle farming or ranching has been tried in many places. In the former, wild turtles and hatchlings are caught and kept in captivity to breed. Subsequent generations can be regarded as captive bred. Ranching does not involve breeding turtles but relies on eggs and hatchlings taken from the wild to be reared in captivity. In some instances a combination of the two methods has been used. Both have also caused controversy. It was reasoned that turtles are extremely nutritious and could help feed the world, and that rearing them for the table was as sensible as farming cattle. Regarding tortoiseshell, hawksbills proved very difficult to rear in captivity, not least because they tended to fight and could cause each other fatal injuries. Green turtles were successful and, furthermore, when fed a high-protein nutritious diet, they matured very quickly producing high-quality, thick scutes, devoid of scratches or blemishes.

The arguments against farming or ranching were the same as for head-starting, as animals still had to be taken from the wild. Though the idea was to release a lot of juveniles to increase the turtle population – in effect, head starting them – the idea of killing any for the table or for decoration became an extremely emotive issue.

The farms and ranches started in many places as small

industries, including in Indonesia, the Philippines, Suriname, the Seychelles, Mexico and a few in the islands of the Torres Straits. But they failed because there were so many problems, such as disease, difficulties with feeding and costs. Two did initially succeed: one on the island of Réunion in the Indian Ocean and one in the Cayman Islands in the western Caribbean.

The most famous of the turtle farms is the one in the Cayman Islands, now called the Cayman Turtle Centre. It was founded in 1968 as Mariculture Ltd. Using predominantly green turtle eggs, hatchlings, juveniles and adults collected and bought legally in Ascension Island, Costa Rica, Guyana and Suriname, and with its good financial backing, it should have been a success. However, emotions took over and adverse advertising in the USA ended with a new law prohibiting the import of any turtle product into the country. With the loss of their biggest market, and with 100,000 turtles to feed, Mariculture declared bankruptcy in 1975.

After that it changed hands a few times and went through more upheavals, as, for example, when Hurricane Michelle washed a large proportion of the turtles away in 2001 – 75 per cent of the breeders were gone and it is said that there were turtles everywhere. The Cayman Turtle Centre is part government owned. It works as a research and education centre and sells turtle meat locally. It also releases yearlings into the wild.

Kelonia, the second turtle farm, is situated on the Island of Réunion, a French department in the Indian Ocean. It, too, was a success initially but faced huge difficulties when the export of products to France was stopped, again due to emotive issues. The cost of running a turtle farm is exorbitant and trade is vital. In spite of the aim to aid research, help conservation and provide food, the farm had to cease trading. Today it is run as a public aquarium and observatory specializing in marine turtles, especially greens (Fig. 16).

Freshwater turtles have also been successfully farmed. Today there is a lot of commercial turtle farming in China where freshwater turtles are raised for consumption and for use in oriental medicines. There persists a local belief that wild-caught turtles are

Fig. 16.
Captive green turtle at Kelonia, Réunion.
STEPHANE CICCIONE

more potent as medicine, so poaching continues and, as a result, wild turtles are under threat. Freshwater turtle farms also trade in the USA where regulations are more successfully maintained. Large-scale marine turtle farming is no longer attempted.

(*See* Appendix I for an overview of conservation and regulatory bodies.)

Chapter 3

What is Tortoiseshell?

Introduction

Tortoiseshell is a natural polymer. It consists of organic molecules called monomers that bind to other monomers to form a long, repeating chain of molecules.

Some polymer chains link together (cross-link) and become what is known as thermosetting when moulded with heat and pressure. This means that they keep their new shape on cooling, but the process can only be done once. Polymers that are thermoplastic, on the other hand, do not cross-link but keep their looser chemical structure, so their shape can be altered again and again by softening them with heat and re-forming them.

There are different types of polymers: natural (as in biological) polymers, such as tortoiseshell, horn and amber; semi-synthetic ones, such as casein or celluloid that use natural materials in combination with chemicals; and completely synthetic ones that have no natural content. Synthetic or semi-synthetic polymers are today usually termed 'plastics'. Early plastics were all semi-synthetic, until the invention of phenol formaldehyde resin (Bakelite) in 1907.

Tortoiseshell has a further characteristic: when heated in a damp atmosphere, its surface becomes colloidal. The result is that thin layers of tortoiseshell can be fused together to form a thicker layer. The welding is permanent. Also, if filed down slightly, the edges of polished tortoiseshell scutes can be fused together to form a larger continuous sheet, such as is used for marquetry.

The Formation of the Keratinous Scutes and their Colour

Turtle scutes are made of a material called keratin. Green and loggerhead turtles have relatively thin scutes on both carapace and plastron, neatly arranged with no overlap. Hawksbills have thicker scutes that are imbricated or overlapping like tiles on a roof – hence the 'imbricata' in the turtle's taxonomic name *Eretmochelys imbricata* (Fig. 17). This allows the scutes to grow thicker – on occasion up to almost 1cm – and give the animal more protection in the coral reef environment. The extra thickness is the main reason for

Fig. 17.
The carapace of a young hawksbill turtle. The animal is being measured, weighed and tagged. Note the overlapping scutes.

the popularity of the hawksbill's tortoiseshell. The females' scutes are often slightly thicker than those of the males'.

Keratin is an insoluble protein, which is very prevalent in the animal kingdom, and is the main constituent of horn, nails, hair, claws, avian beaks, rhinoceros horn, baleen, pangolin scales, porcupine quills and more. It is also present in skin.

There are two types of keratin: alpha-keratin (α-keratin) and beta-keratin (β-keratin), the former is found mostly in mammals, birds and reptiles, and the latter only in birds and reptiles. The composition of turtle scutes is complex, consisting mainly of β-keratin with a small amount of α-keratin plus a very small mineral content. The first scutes on a hatchling are soft α-keratin, enabling it to curl up in the egg, but these are shed at a young age as the proper scutes start to grow. From then on, the scutes may be worn down through wear and tear, but they are never shed.

The two types of keratin form in different ways: a helical structure in α-keratin and a minutely pleated sheet structure in β-keratin. Neither is visible to the naked eye, but only under very high magnification.

Fig. 18.
Underside of an unpolished hawksbill turtle's carapacial scute. Note the clearly visible wavy growth lines.

Turtle scutes are formed by cells in the dermis covering the bone and cartilage of the animal's skeleton. They are not laid down in smooth, regular layers but can be irregular, giving rise to the wavy pattern on the surface that is especially visible on the rough, reverse side of a raw scute (Fig. 18). Most marine creatures have a film of slippery liquid covering their bodies that helps them to be more energy efficient in the water, but turtles lack this. It is possible that the microscopic folds in the keratin layers enable algae to attach themselves to the turtle, giving it a slippery surface and making it more hydrodynamic (Fig. 19).

Fig. 19. ▲
Green turtle foraging near Barbados. Its pale plastron is coloured by algae.

As a hawksbill turtle grows and each keratin layer in a scute forms fractionally larger than the previous layer, it grows forward, pushing under the scute in front and lifting it from the dermis, resulting in the imbrication or overlap. The imbrication does not start until the hatchling is about three months old and is very pronounced in juveniles. When the turtle reaches full size, the scutes cease to grow in area but continue to grow in thickness, so they do not produce further imbrication. In old animals, the overlap can be worn away to the extent that it is no longer obvious. The scutes on the plastron always get worn, so do not display any noticeable imbrication.

There seems to be a slight difference in the compactness of the structure of the keratin in the tortoiseshell from each of the three species. When an extremely thin slice is taken vertically through the scute and viewed under very high magnification, it would appear that the loggerhead's is the most compact, which may account for the fact that it is the most difficult to work with, especially when moulding it. The green turtle's keratin appears to have a slightly less compact structure and has been used much more than that of the loggerhead. The hawksbill's displays a looser structure, which would explain why it is the preferred material with which to work, and why it moulds more easily (*see* Chapter 6).

The colour in the carapacial scutes that gives rise to the mottled effect is due to melanin, which is one of the most common natural pigments in the animal kingdom. Most keratins owe their colour to melanin, including human skin and hair. It is produced by cells called melanocytes situated in the dermis. The scutes' melanin is laid down on each separate layer of keratin as minute grains. As each successive layer is formed and more melanin is laid down, the effect is one of patches of colour, which, seen under magnification, penetrate the tortoiseshell in a pattern of microscopic, fuzzy-looking blobs. The young hatchling's scutes are dark, but as the turtle grows, there are areas of the dermis that do not have melanocytes and, therefore, produce a material lacking in strong colour but of a pale golden hue. Further, melanocytes can cease production or suddenly start producing pigment. In the latter event, the patch of colour appears like a shadow in the tortoiseshell. The reason for the arrest and restart of melanin production is unknown, but there is a theory that it could be influenced by ambient temperature, as is the production of keratin.

During the years when the turtle grows, the scutes become larger, growing both in width and length. This happens from the posterior, so successive dark patches of melanin may occur as lines radiating from the back of each scute. As the turtle ages, its carapace becomes more domed, so the scutes grow more in some directions than in others. This can also affect the pattern of the mottling.

Fig. 20.
Polished carapacial scute from a hawksbill showing the mottled pattern of pigmentation.

The pattern in the carapacial scutes of hawksbill and green turtles is usually very beautiful, ranging in colours from pale amber through reddish brown to almost black (Fig. 20). The loggerhead's carapace is more heavily pigmented and darker in colour, with less obvious mottling. In spite of it being considered less attractive than the others, it has been used in the past, as the archives of both the Louvre in Paris and the Rijksmuseum in Amsterdam can attest.

The tortoiseshell on the plastron of all three turtles is pale with no dark patches, as there are no melanocytes in the dermis (Fig. 21). The different colours of the carapace and the plastron are believed to be camouflage. The carapace of a swimming turtle viewed from above by a predator will blend into the dark seabed, whereas if viewed from beneath, the turtle's pale belly will be less visible against the paler water and sky above (Fig. 22).

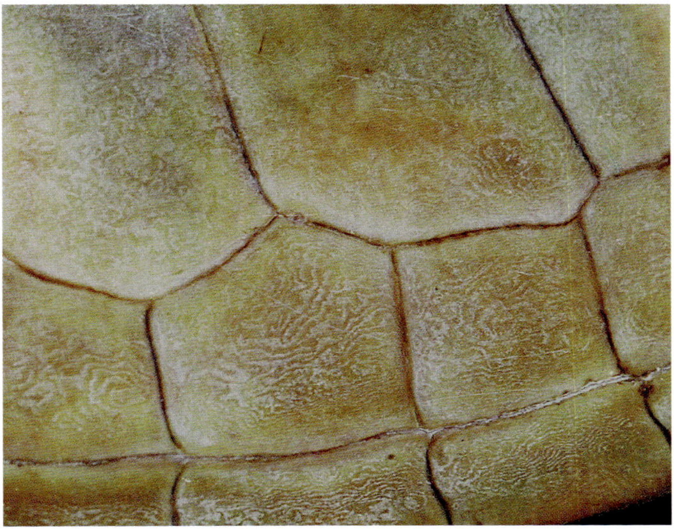

Fig. 21.
Detail of the pale plastron of a hawksbill turtle, showing the lack of imbrication and the wavy growth lines.

Fig. 22.
Whole, unpolished scute from the centre of a hawksbill's carapace. Note the scratches and marks from a barnacle, as well as the layered edge caused by imbrication.

If a scute is severely damaged or cracked, for example, by a barnacle, or if it is lost, the dermis can produce more keratin and repair it, even growing a new one. Replaced scutes lack mottling and imbrication.

In the case of farmed green turtles, the animals grow much faster than they would in the wild, and their scutes grow much thicker with clear colours and beautiful mottling due to the diet fed to the captive turtles. When they reach maturity, their scutes gradually become thin again and resemble more those of a wild green turtle.

Chapter 4

Identifying Tortoiseshell and its Simulants

Natural Materials

Horn and Baleen

Tortoiseshell is composed mainly of keratin, a protein that is very common in the animal kingdom and is one of the main constituents of animal anatomy.

In the world of decorative arts, there are many materials that derive from animals and are made of keratin; for example, tortoiseshell, horn, rhino horn, claws, hooves, birds' beaks, feathers, human hair, animal fur, wool, whale baleen, pangolin scales and more (*see* Chapter 8). It is also present in skin.

Of all these, only two might be confused with tortoiseshell: horn and baleen. The two materials have different structures but both can be moulded into shape using heat and pressure because, like tortoiseshell, they are thermoplastic. After treating horn and baleen with heat and pressure, they are difficult to tell apart as their typical structures are altered by the treatment.

Horn comes from members of the family Bovidae, which is a large group comprising animals as disparate as antelopes and bison. It grows in many different shapes and sizes. The horn used to imitate tortoiseshell is most likely to be a large one of simple shape, such as ox horn. The material grows on the head of the animal, as a covering to a bony protuberance.

The keratin in horn is laid down in sheets as a laminate. Because of its structure, horn has a slightly striated appearance and can appear fibrous. This is not very visible in black horns but immediately becomes noticeable in horn of varying hues, such as ox horn. The colour in horn is, like tortoiseshell, caused by grains of the pigment melanin (Fig. 23).

Horn is the most common simulant or substitute for tortoiseshell. As it is made principally of keratin, it reacts in much the same way as tortoiseshell in most tests and is also best identified by sight.

Horn has been used to bulk out tortoiseshell as it was a far less expensive material (Figs. 24 and 25), and it is believed that baleen was used in the same way, especially in the production of small boxes that were mass produced, ready for decoration with a thin

Fig. 23.
Detail of ox horn, showing the fibrous-looking structure and the pigmentation following the striations (magnified).

Fig. 24.
Front of a brooch (damaged) with a tortoiseshell surface. The brooch is mostly horn.

Fig. 25.
Underside of the brooch showing the tortoiseshell to have been bulked out with horn. (Brooch fittings missing.)

Fig. 26.
Small horn box with a thin layer of tortoiseshell on the top of the lid. Note the laminated structure is reappearing in the horn base.

layer of tortoiseshell. With age, the laminated and striated structure of horn may become visible (Fig. 26).

Dyed horn can emulate another material: for example, it makes a good imitation of jet when dyed black. It can also be given a mottled pattern to imitate tortoiseshell. Various pigments have been used to achieve this effect; one of the most successful today is commercially available hair dye, which is already formulated to dye keratin (Figs. 27 and 28).

Boiling horn in nitric acid gives it a yellow hue and, after careful washing and neutralizing, it is painted on the surface. The colour only penetrates slightly, whereas in tortoiseshell the pigmentation goes all the way through, but if painted several times with a weak mixture, thus unevenly building up the patches to the required density of colour, painted horn can be convincing.

Horn has also been used to imitate tortoiseshell piqué brooches. When viewed by strong transmitted light, there is no indication of mottling, the piqué is coarser than it would be in a finer piece made of tortoiseshell and the metal used is less expensive – probably silver rather than gold (Fig. 29).

Fig. 27. ▲
Horn box. The top and base have been painted to imitate tortoiseshell.

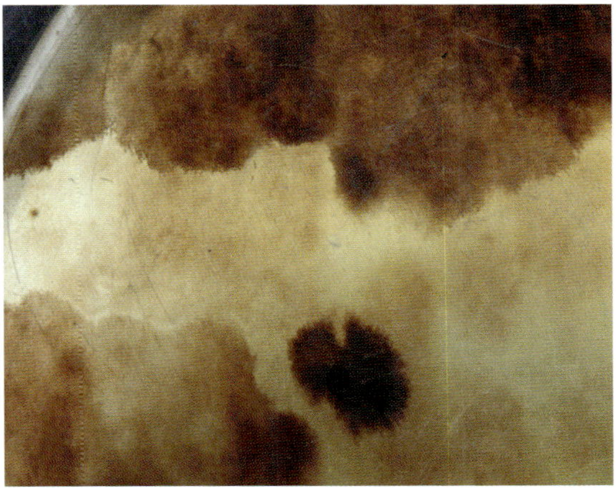

Fig. 28. ►
Detail of the colouring on the horn box. Note the defined outline of the colours, which do not penetrate the material.

Baleen comes from the Mysticeti or baleen whales, that is, the ones without teeth, of which there are fifteen species, including bowheads, humpbacks and the largest of all whales, the blue whale. Baleen grows in the upper jaw of the animal and hangs in curtains of hundreds of overlapping plates, which are used as a sieve to catch the shrimp and plankton on which the whales live. Depending on the size of the whale, the plates can be up to 4m long and grow continuously, but are worn away with use, resulting in a fringe of bristles.

Baleen is found in a variety of colours similar to those of horn and is likewise coloured by melanin. The material is like horn in very many ways, though it has a different structure. It consists of tubes of keratin stacked in a keratin matrix, sandwiched between plates of keratin. As with horn, the structure is lost when baleen is pressed or moulded. (For more information on horn and baleen, *see* Chapter 8.)

Fig. 29.
Horn piqué brooch, copying the popular tortoiseshell ones. The piqué is less delicate and the metal less expensive. The diameter of the brooch is 4cm.

Pen Shell (Fig 30)

There is one organic material that is not keratinous but which has been, on occasion, confused with tortoiseshell: the pen shell (*Pinna nobilis*), a large marine bivalve mollusc in the order Pteriida.

When polished it may resemble tortoiseshell in its colouring and pattern, though careful inspection will soon show that the pattern is not that of a turtle scute. The *Pinna* shell is composed mainly of calcium carbonate and, as a result, is heavier than tortoiseshell. Being largely mineralized, it is also cold to the touch.

Fig. 30.
Section of a necklace with a disc of pen shell (**Pinna nobilis**), which could be mistaken for tortoiseshell.

Early Plastics Used to Imitate Tortoiseshell

Celluloid (Cellulose Nitrate)

Celluloid was created in about 1860 by Alexander Parkes and was originally called Parkesine. It was based on plant matter from cotton or wood that was chemically modified with nitric acid plus sulphuric acid and plasticized with camphor. It was a revolutionary product and made an excellent tortoiseshell imitation, as well as a good base for the light-sensitive coating in the production of photographic cine film, because it was possible to produce celluloid in a form that was not rigid. It did, however, have certain disadvantages, the main one being that it was highly inflammable.

Celluloid tends to degrade after a time and when the process starts it is unstoppable. The item slowly crumbles and falls to bits, emitting a smell of camphor as it does so. At the first sign of this, it should be isolated from any other celluloid items, as any contamination can set the process off in otherwise perfectly stable

▲ Fig. 31.
Plastic imitation of Spanish *peineta*. Although a good imitation of tortoiseshell, the mottling is too distinct and tends to be on the surface. The comb is celluloid and may be at risk of degrading.

pieces. Celluloid should never be stored in sealed containers, as this hastens its deterioration.

Tortoiseshell imitations made from plastics copy the mottling with streaks and swirls of colour, rather than patches. The edges of the dark areas are more sharply defined than those of the natural material (Figs. 31–37).

Care should be taken when testing celluloid as the hot point test can be dangerous due to the material's combustibility. If a small scraping is taken from an inconspicuous area and burned, it will smell acrid. It is possible to use the hot water alternative, in which case celluloid will emit a slight smell of camphor, but this can only be used if the item has no metal or other parts.

Laboratory tests give good results with celluloid, which is identifiable by Fourier Transform Infrared Spectroscopy (FTIR) (*see* Chapter 5).

Fig. 32.
Plastic box imitating tortoiseshell. Note the swirly pattern of the colouring and its clearly defines edges.

Fig. 33.
Tortoiseshell box. Note the 'soft' appearance of the mottling.

Celluloid is still used today to imitate tortoiseshell and is manufactured in blocks or sheets. The latter can be heat moulded. It is also produced as a laminate on an acrylic backing.

'Non-Flam' Celluloid (Cellulose Acetate)

In order to overcome the problem of inflammability, a similar product was marketed in 1894 using acetic acid instead of nitric acid. Originally it was used as dope on aircraft wings, but after World War I, it was discovered that it could be made into a fibre that could be woven.

Cellulose acetate could also be moulded, but in early years it tended to shrink and distort in the process, though the problem was later solved. Like celluloid, it can also degrade and gives off an acrid, vinegary smell. It will do the same when tested using heat.

Also, like celluloid, cellulose acetate can be easily identified in a laboratory by tests such as FTIR (*see* Chapter 5). It is still produced today as a tortoiseshell imitation and sold in blocks.

Casein

Casein is a milk protein. The early plastic by the same name was invented at the start of the twentieth century and marketed under various names, including Casein, Galalith and Erinoid.

The protein casein was reacted with formaldehyde to make a hard material, which was produced in blocks and could be machined. It was hygroscopic and could be dyed, making it suitable for the production of buttons. It was a popular choice in the manufacture of fountain pens.

Casein does not degrade in the same way as the cellulose-based plastics, but it can craze on the surface. When tested with a hot point, it gives off a smell of burnt milk.

Under UV light, pale areas of casein fluoresce a bright, chalky colour, which can seem similar to the chalky fluorescence of the pale areas of tortoiseshell, though the definition between light and dark areas is more pronounced.

When testing in a laboratory and seeking to identify tortoiseshell or a simulant, casein is the one plastic that can present problems because it gives very similar results to tortoiseshell, horn and other keratins in many of the simpler laboratory tests. It may prove necessary to use more advanced tests, such as mass spectrometry (*see* Chapter 5).

Other Plastics Used to Imitate Tortoiseshell

The early plastics made good imitations of tortoiseshell and they are still in production today. Many of the problems with instability or combustibility have been solved. There are also other plastics on the market of which the following three types are probably the best known. Compared to the previously mentioned ones, which are termed 'early plastics', these are regarded as new, although they are now themselves quite old.

The plastics industry continues to evolve and further types are being discovered. It is likely that they will also be used to imitate the most popular items that are made with simulated tortoiseshell, such as spectacle frames, combs and hair ornaments, but no plastic imitation has as yet been produced that successfully mimics the pigmentation in tortoiseshell (*see* Chapter 3).

Acrylic

Poly(methyl methacrylate) (PMMA), also known as acrylic, plexiglass, Perspex and several other names, was invented in the mid-1930s. During World War II it was used to make lightweight but optically clear and strong canopies for aircraft cockpits. It is a thermoplastic, so it can be bent into shape with heat and pressure.

Acrylic is produced in sheet form and in blocks or rods to imitate tortoiseshell. It is sometimes used as a firm backing for a different material with a pattern resembling tortoiseshell.

Polyester

Polyester is a versatile thermoplastic. When mixed with glass fibre, it can be made into large mouldings and used in, for example, the construction of boats. It was first used in the 1940s.

As a tortoiseshell imitation it is used without a filler and is generally produced in rod or block form for further manufacture.

▲ Fig. 34.
Plastic bangle imitating tortoiseshell. It has become brittle, prior to degrading.

PVC

Polyvinyl chloride was first used in the 1920s, but it was perfected twenty years later and since then has been one of the most useful and popular plastics. It can be produced in either flexible or rigid forms and is used for everything from plastic sheeting and clothes to furniture, though it can degrade if subjected to too much UV light. As a tortoiseshell imitation it is mostly used in sheet form.

Fig. 35. ►
Detail of the typical pattern of the pigmentation in tortoiseshell, which is made up of multi-layered keratin, each layer coloured by minute grains of melanin.

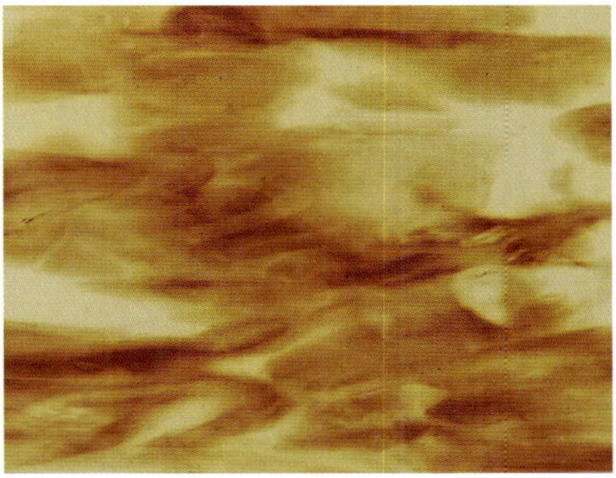

Fig. 36. ►
Detail of typical plastic tortoiseshell simulant, showing the colouring in swirls with well-defined edges.

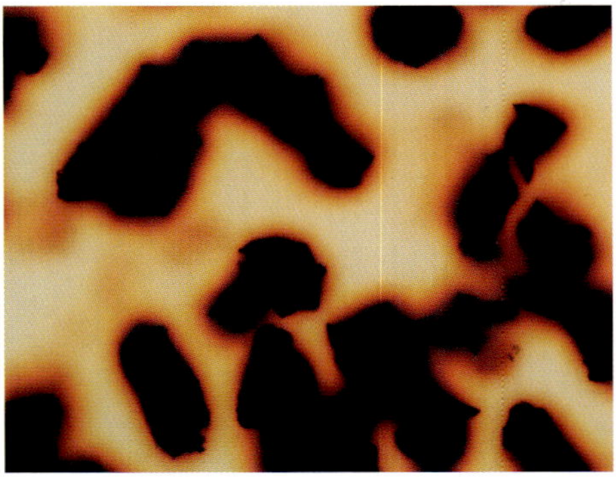

Fig. 37. ►
Another form of plastic tortoiseshell simulant. The pattern is formed of dark blobs surrounded by a haze of colour in the pale material.

Visual Identification of Tortoiseshell and its Imitations

Common sense is a useful tool when identifying an object. For example, it would be very unusual to find horn or plastic made into some of the more luxurious items, such as carved card cases or silver-mounted dressing-table sets. The following is a brief guide of what to look out for.

Initial Impressions

- The use of gold piqué work is indicative of tortoiseshell, as is the quality of workmanship. This is especially helpful with blond tortoiseshell.
- Occasionally, an item is stamped on the base with its origin or other mark. This is not often done to tortoiseshell. Even masterpieces, such as the Neapolitan piqué work, were seldom signed.

Fig. 38.
Moiré silk effect of wavy growth lines reappearing on tortoiseshell surface as it dulls with age or over-exposure to UV light or damp.

Fig. 39.
The surface of the tortoiseshell degrades further from the moiré silk effect to become uneven and the colour darkens.

- The moiré silk effect of wavy lines on the surface of smooth but slightly dulled material (caused by the growth lines in the tortoiseshell reappearing) is unique to tortoiseshell, and copies in plastic are crude and easily identifiable as fakes. In badly degraded material, the surface of the tortoiseshell is no longer smooth (Figs. 38–40).
- Colour on the surface only is indicative of plastic or possibly horn (Figs. 41 and 42).
- A fibrous-looking structure indicates horn.
- Swirls of colour in the material indicate a plastic imitation.
- Very dark blobs of colour may indicate a plastic imitation, but further inspection is required (Figs. 43 and 44).
- Plastic is lighter than tortoiseshell or horn. Very rarely is it made with a filler to give it weight when copying tortoiseshell.

▲ Fig. 40.
Plastic box imitating the wavy growth lines of tortoiseshell. Note that the box has also begun to degrade and the plastic has begun to blister.

▼ Fig. 41.
Plastic hair comb imitating tortoiseshell. The pattern has been painted and is only on the surface. Note the clear edges of the 'carving'.

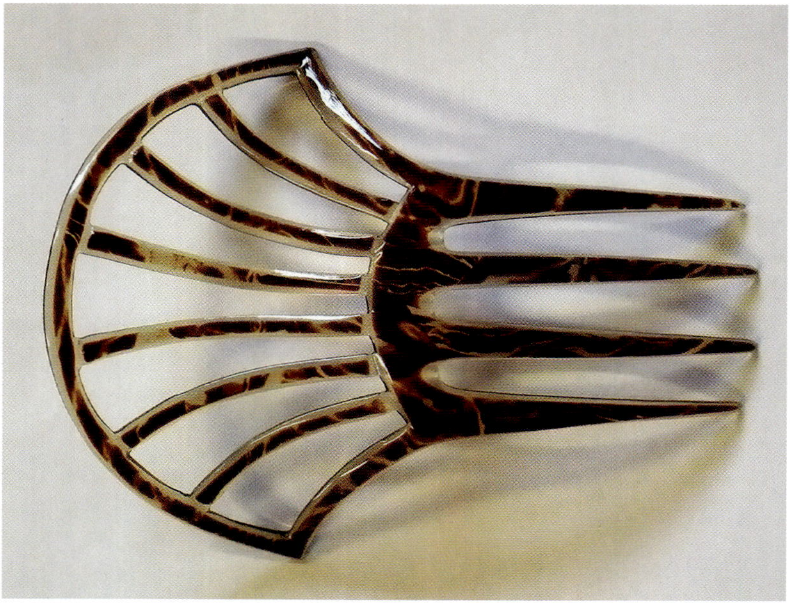

▲ Fig. 42.
Horn box with a painted tortoiseshell pattern. Note the sharply defined edges of the mottling.

Fig. 43. ►
Plastic imitation tortoiseshell snuff bottle. The colouring is too well defined. Another indication that it is a fake is that the carving penetrates the material so it could not hold snuff.

Fig. 44.
Detail of a less common pattern on tortoiseshell, which could be confused with plastic. Viewed under higher magnification the grains of pigment become visible.

Further Inspection

- When viewed by transmitted light and with a 10× lens, the patches in tortoiseshell appear as minute specs of colour, closely packed and penetrating the material, giving the impression of fuzzy blobs of colour.
- Air bubbles are indicative of plastic.
- Patterns in relief that have soft, rounded edges are pressed. It could be tortoiseshell, horn or plastic (Fig. 45).
- Patterns in relief with crisp edges are carved. It is likely to be tortoiseshell, though it could be horn (Fig. 46).
- Slight flaking at the edge of an item suggests tortoiseshell veneer. Horn seldom flakes in thin layers. Plastics do not flake.
- Signs of degrading indicate an early plastic. Tortoiseshell does not crumble (unless extremely old), but will go dull and appear darker.
- Small areas that appear to be chipped may, on closer inspection, reveal themselves to have been gnawed by insects, such as

clothes' moth larvae. Tortoiseshell, horn and plastics seldom chip around the edge, but both tortoiseshell and horn can be attacked by moths (Fig. 47).

Fig. 45. ►
Detail of surface of tortoiseshell card case pictured in Fig. 94. The rounded edges to the pattern show that it has been pressed.

Fig. 46. ►
Detail of the surface of a tortoiseshell card case pictured in Fig 94. The sharp edges to the pattern show that it has been carved. Note also the marks from the carving tool.

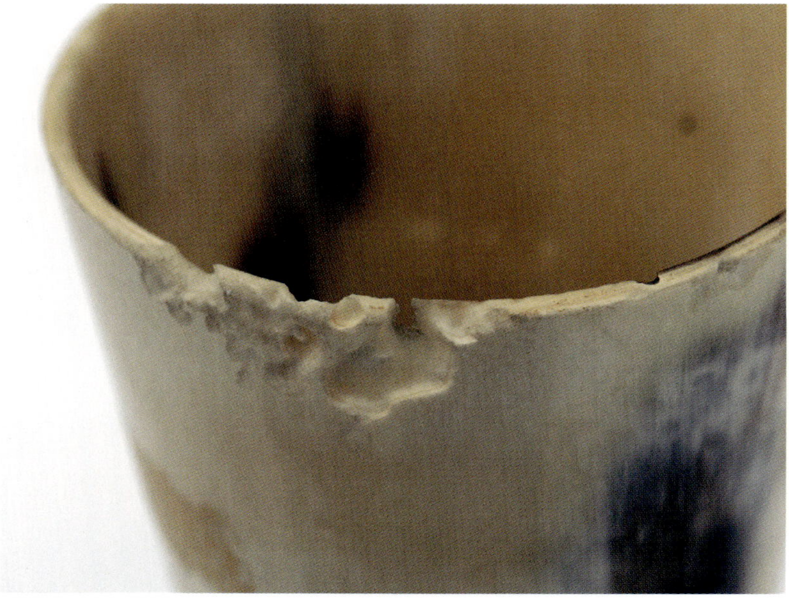

Fig. 47.
Detail of the edge of a horn beaker, which has been attacked by insects, probably clothes moths.

Simple Testing

- Under crossed polarizing filters, a rainbow of colours in a very fine pattern is indicative of tortoiseshell. Horn displays a similar pattern.
- Under crossed polarizing filters, large patches, blocks or swirls of colour are all indicative of plastic. None of them resemble the fine-coloured pattern of tortoiseshell.
- Under long-wave UV light, pale areas of tortoiseshell, horn and casein fluoresce a chalky colour, but their structure or patterning may appear more clearly defined, plus aiding differentiation (*see also* pages 76–80).

Chapter 5

Testing Tortoiseshell

Introduction

As with all gem materials, the first and most important test for tortoiseshell is observation. Indeed, tortoiseshell is one of the materials that can usually be identified by sight, especially with the help of a gemmologist's 10× lens and transmitted light. Tortoiseshell's most common simulant is horn, and as both materials are made of keratin they can give almost identical results in many tests. A person who deals with both materials can tell them apart by feel or by gently tapping them against the teeth – tortoiseshell is said to feel softer than horn, and to sound different; however, such a test could only be undertaken by someone with a great deal of experience of the two materials.

Tortoiseshell can feel a little like plastic. Both are warm to the touch and neither is heavy. No imitations are coloured by areas made up of masses of minute spots throughout the material, but tend to be coloured only on the surface (both plastic and painted horn can display this), or have swirls or blobs of colour throughout that were produced in the molten plastic. No tortoiseshell would have air bubbles in it, as might plastic.

Tortoiseshell is the only material to display the areas of wavy lines that are the original growth lines and which reappear as the surface dulls, and immediately identifies the material as being tortoiseshell. Attempts have been made, unsuccessfully, to copy the phenomenon with a surface pattern in plastic (Figs. 38 and 40).

More difficulties may arise when dealing with dark tortoiseshell, where it is difficult to shine a light through it to see the mottling, or with blond tortoiseshell that is a plain honey-colour and devoid of mottling. There can be occasions when further testing is necessary.

As well as tortoiseshell and horn reacting in many ways to give almost identical test results, a semi-synthetic plastic, casein, can also give very similar results in some laboratory tests.

Simple Tests

Polarizing Filters (Crossed Polars)

A polariscope consists of two polarizing filters parallel to each other with a light below. The upper filter can rotate. The item to be tested is placed between the filters and the top one rotated. When the filters are in the crossed position, no light can pass through, so the top one appears black (extinction). As it disturbs the direction of the light beam, a sample placed between the filters can redirect the light, thus allowing some to pass through and displaying a pattern that aids identification. It can also show up stress in a material.

◄ Fig. 48.
Mottled tortoiseshell viewed under crossed polars (magnified). Note the rainbow of colours in a striated pattern in the pale areas.

Fig. 49. Blond tortoiseshell viewed under crossed polars (magnified). Note the rainbow of colours in a striated pattern.

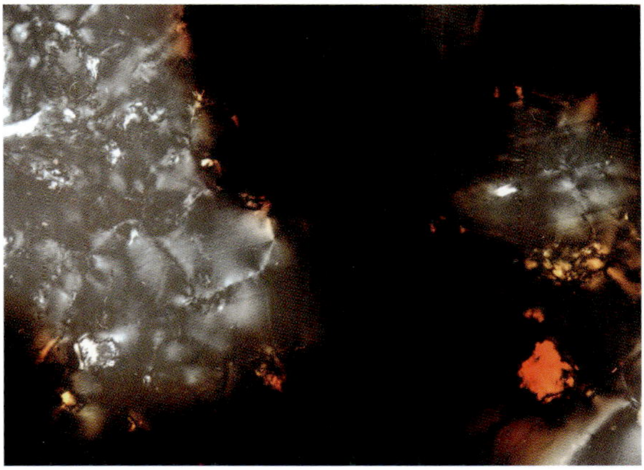

Fig. 50. A plastic viewed under crossed polars (magnified). Note the blocks and patches of colour.

Fig. 51. A different plastic viewed under crossed polars (magnified). The surface is partly incised causing the dark lines. Note the large areas of colour.

◄ Fig. 52. Pale horn viewed under crossed polars (magnified). Note the similarity to the pattern observed in tortoiseshell.

A sample to be examined can be too large to fit on to a polariscope, in which case it is possible to carry out the test with two polarizing filters and a light.

Crossed polars give a very good indication of the nature of the material. This is particularly useful when identifying blond tortoiseshell, which can look a lot like plastic.

Tortoiseshell transmits some light throughout a 360-degree turn of one of the polarizing filters. There is no extinction, but a rainbow of colours can be seen in a striated pattern in the blond area of tortoiseshell (Figs. 48 and 49). If the item has been bent or moulded, then there may be some stress in the material, which will show as a disturbance in the pattern.

Some plastics are inert and show nothing under crossed polars. Some display irregular dark and light patches, while others display swirls of colour. The differences are due to the number of different plastics used and also to their method of production. None display the rainbow effect of tortoiseshell (Figs. 50 and 51).

Horn is seldom transparent enough to be tested using crossed polars. Very pale and translucent horn displays a pattern similar to that of the pale areas of tortoiseshell, but the horn's natural colour is more silvery than that of tortoiseshell and lacks the honey-coloured hue. (Fig. 52)

Ultra-Violet (UV) Light

UV light is sometimes called 'black light' as it is not visible to the human eye. It is a radiation in the electro-magnetic spectrum, which has a shorter wavelength than visible light but longer than X-ray. Testing must be carried out in a darkened place in order to see the full effect.

By illuminating an item with UV light it is possible to see whether it absorbs the light and remains inert or whether it re-emits it on another visible wavelength (fluoresces in UV) and, if so, what colour it is. Different colours can aid in identification.

Gemmologists use both long-wave and short-wave UV light (LWUV and SWUV). Tortoiseshell reacts in much the same way to both, but more strongly to long wave. The dark areas may fluoresce with a slight 'bloom' or may remain inert. The pale areas fluoresce with a pale, chalky colour, sometimes with hints of blue. As tortoiseshell is often backed in some way with another material it can be difficult to judge the colour of the fluorescence, as the material backing it may affect the result. In the case of an ivory box lined with tortoiseshell, the ivory's fluorescence can show through. If backed with wood, tortoiseshell can fluoresce a chalky beige colour.

Horn can fluoresce the same way as tortoiseshell, as can some plastic imitations, notably casein, which fluoresces strongly in the pale areas, although dark areas remain inert. Nonetheless, UV is a useful test and can give some good indications. Under UV the striated pattern in horn can show up more clearly, while the dark areas of painted horn are less clear than those of tortoiseshell. In a fluorescing plastic, the dark and light areas become very clearly defined.

Hot Point Test

The hot point test consists of burning a small area of the item with a metal point and evaluating its reaction, both whether it melts or burns, and what kind of aroma it emits. It is a destructive test as it will leave a mark on the item. Further, it is not without danger, as one of the tortoiseshell imitations is 'celluloid' (cellulose nitrate), which is highly combustible. Celluloid was the most common tortoiseshell simulant used in the first half of the twentieth century.

To avoid the danger, it is possible to take a very small scraping from an inconspicuous place on the item and burn that, but this is also destructive. Nonetheless, the hot point test can provide a lot of information. Tortoiseshell burns with a smell like burning hair. Among the early plastics that were much used to imitate tortoiseshell, cellulose nitrate smells of camphor, cellulose acetate smells of vinegar and casein smells of burnt milk. Newer plastics, such as polyester, have an acrid smell. Unfortunately, horn, like tortoiseshell, smells of burnt hair because they both consist of keratin, as does hair.

An alternative method of testing by heat is to place the object for testing into hot water. Although it avoids any risk of fire if the object is celluloid, and is not directly destructive, the type of item that can be submerged in hot water is extremely limited as it cannot be used on anything in a mount or similar. Most plastics give off the same aroma as if touched with a hot point, though much fainter. Tortoiseshell and horn do not give off any aroma. Further, if the temperature of the water is not strictly controlled and becomes too hot, there is a risk of tortoiseshell softening, losing shape and becoming cloudy.

Specific Gravity (SG) and Refractive Index (RI)

Specific gravity and refractive index are tests much used by gemmologists for small, mineral specimens. SG measures the relative density of a material to that of an equal volume of water and RI measures the amount a sample bends a light beam passing through it. They are excellent indicators of identity for gemstones.

Neither test is of much practical help when investigating items thought to be made of tortoiseshell. Not only are the tests extremely difficult to perform on anything large, but the items can be damaged by the tests. For example, to test for the SG of an item larger than a gemstone, the hydrostatic method would have to be used, which involves immersing the whole item in water. The liquids used for testing RI could damage an item. The resulting figures or 'constants' for tortoiseshell are, in any case, similar to those of plastics.

Hardness and Sectility

Hardness is a valuable gemmological test that can aid in the identification of gem materials, notably minerals. It is measured on a scale called Mohs scale from 1 to 10, with 1 being the softest and 10 the hardest (which is diamond). It determines how hard materials are in comparison to each other. It is of little use when identifying tortoiseshell.

Sectility refers to the way in which a material can be cut. As with hardness, it is of little relevance in the identification of tortoiseshell, which, like horn, can easily be carved or filed with the appropriate tools.

Advanced Testing

In the majority of cases it is possible to identify tortoiseshell by sight or by simple tests. It is usually sufficient to know that an item is tortoiseshell and not necessary to know from which species it derives. Nevertheless, it is possible to encounter a few excellent imitations of tortoiseshell, or a tortoiseshell item that is so dark or thick that it is not possible to identify it with certainty either by sight or simple tests. On these occasions, it may be necessary to resort to more advanced testing in a laboratory.

There are also circumstances when it would be good to know which species of turtle has been used to make an object. Today this can also be investigated.

There are drawbacks to many of the tests. Most call for a tiny sample to be taken, which is destructive, even if the sample is minute. Owners of antiques would seldom be keen to allow a small hole to be drilled in something of value, although, of course, when it is necessary to carry out such a test, the sample is always taken from an inconspicuous area. Another drawback to the advanced tests is that large objects probably cannot be moved to a laboratory, nor will they fit into any testing machines.

A further complication is that horn and tortoiseshell often give almost identical results because they are both made of keratin. Among tortoiseshell imitations, casein can also give results that are similar to tortoiseshell and horn because it is a protein-based, semi-synthetic plastic. Other plastics are easily identifiable by laboratory tests as they are not protein-based.

Fourier-Transform Infrared Spectroscopy (FTIR)

FTIR is a favourite gemmological laboratory test. It measures the reaction of a specimen to different frequencies in the infra-red spectrum, which is part of the electro-magnetic spectrum. The results are calibrated by a computer and give a reading of the specimen's absorption of the light at each wavelength.

The test results are compared with a known database. They give clear indication when a sample is of a totally different composition, such as plastic, but they can have difficulty distinguishing between tortoiseshell and horn. Casein also gives very similar results.

FTIR is a destructive test when a small sample is taken for the reading, but non-destructive variations of the test exist, though their results are not always quite as accurate.

Specular Reflectance IR Spectroscopy

This is a variation of FTIR, in which the beam of light goes through a microscopically thin amount of the surface of the sample, and is reflected back out again, registering information on its composition on the way. It does not necessitate taking a sample and so is not destructive. Further, with the addition of a simple accessory, it is possible to test large objects. It can also be used on items that are made up, for example, tortoiseshell boxes with wooden carcasses such as tea caddies, though they must have a high polish, which is not always the case with old tortoiseshell items. Any lacquer or oils on the surface can distort the results.

Visual Near Infra-Red Spectroscopy (Vis-NIR)

Vis-NIR is another variation that uses a light source of a longer wavelength, near the infra-red wavelengths.

Raman Spectroscopy

Raman spectroscopy works in a slightly different way to FTIR spectroscopy. It uses monochromatic light and laser beams to excite the molecules in a sample to record how the particles are scattered and altered when they are hit. The test is non-destructive and appears to be able to differentiate more easily between the proteins, giving clearer results for casein and a better indication of whether an item is horn or tortoiseshell.

Proteomics

Today more advanced methods are being discovered and developed. Proteomics is becoming more and more used and is taking over from other methods of testing, because it gives more and detailed answers.

Proteomics is the study of proteins, which are an important part of living organisms. They are made up of amino acids, which combine in different ways to form a multitude of proteins, each with its own role; for example, for the structure, function, DNA replication, and regulation of tissues and organs.

Proteomics can be used in many different ways, including in the identification of organisms by studying the composition, configuration and activity of proteins present. There are various ways of studying proteins, but the processes are complicated and can only be performed in a specialized laboratory.

Mass-spectrometry (MS) covers several forms of test. Tortoiseshell is successfully tested using LC-MS/MS, which is the combination of liquid chromatography (LC) with mass spectrometry (MS). It not only differentiates between tortoiseshell and horn, but it can also identify the species of turtle from which the tortoiseshell was derived.

The test is termed micro-destructive because it requires that a tiny sample be removed from the object being tested. In general practice, it is not usually necessary to go into the details of the species, as it is sufficient to know that something is tortoiseshell and not horn or a simulant, but by using proteomics it is now possible to identify archaeological and degraded items, as well as fresh ones. It is, therefore, of great value in the academic world.

Zooarchaeological mass spectrometry (ZooMS) is another form of MS, which is gaining popularity because it is fast and can test many samples in a short time. Further, it can test archaeological items, such as bones, because the collagen content degrades slowly. It is not suitable for keratins as they degrade too fast, but it can be used on ancient turtle bones. Thus, today it would be possible to identify some of the turtle bone fragments in burial finds mentioned in Chapter 7, which have hitherto not been identifiable unless there was a whole skeleton present and the identification could be based on the morphology of the animal, which was often inaccurate.

DNA Testing

In order to discover the species from which tortoiseshell derived, it is possible to test for DNA. It is a slightly destructive test, as a very small sample of material must be removed to carry it out. In the case of marquetry, it would be very difficult to perform as the material being tested would be very thin and a sample must be taken from inside the material in order to avoid any contamination. Surface cleaning is not enough. Today mass spectrometry would be more likely to be used instead.

DNA testing has, however, been carried out with success on illegal and poached tortoiseshell, aiding in law enforcement. Raw scutes are of sufficient thickness to ensure a result, and having to make a tiny hole in a scute is of less importance.

Mitochondrial DNA (mtDNA) has proved very useful for testing live turtles to discover their relationship to each other, which has given insight into their nesting and foraging habits and localities (*see* Chapter 2).

Radiocarbon or Carbon 14 Testing (^{14}C)

Carbon 14 analysis measures the amount of radiocarbon absorbed by a living organism. All living organisms contain carbon, most of which is stable, but a very small amount – the isotope called ^{14}C or radiocarbon – is not stable and is radioactive. It starts to degrade the moment the organism dies.

The amount of ^{14}C in the atmosphere has a 'half-life' of 5,730 years; that is, it halves in that time, halves again in another 5,730 years and so forth. On the basis of this, it is possible to judge from the amount of ^{14}C in the organism when it died and stopped the absorption.

The results are not very precise for before the mid-twentieth century, but after that it can give a much more exact estimate. This is due to atmospheric nuclear detonations, which doubled the amounts of ^{14}C across the biosphere. It is sometimes referred to as bomb carbon 14 testing.

The ^{14}C content in tortoiseshell is affected by the so-called marine reservoir effect, which means that anything from the sea appears to be about 400 years older when compared to material from the land of the same age. Corrections can be made to accommodate the phenomenon, but to do that it is necessary to know where the turtle lived and where it sourced its food. Due to turtle migration, that is seldom possible, so results may be inaccurate. Also, ^{14}C readings can vary by up to forty years from the northern to the southern hemispheres, hence the importance of knowing from where the species comes.

Also, while ^{14}C testing might be used to give an indication of when a turtle died, it cannot necessarily tell when an item of tortoiseshell was made because the tortoiseshell may have been stockpiled before use.

The series of ^{14}C tests carried out on the scutes of a recently deceased hawksbill turtle to try to determine its age would not be affected by this, as the age of death was known and the subsequent ages of the scutes in one animal would give dates backwards from that point (*see* Chapter 1).

As with many other tests, ^{14}C is slightly destructive, as a small sample must be extracted for testing and, to avoid contamination, the sample must be taken from inside the specimen. It is not sufficient to clean the surface.

Chapter 6

Treatments and Care

Introduction

Tortoiseshell is a natural polymer or plastic, and is 'thermoplastic' (*see* Chapter 3). It is a very versatile material, as it can be cut, moulded, welded to itself to form thick or long pieces, carved, dyed and bleached.

Basic Moulding

Turtle scutes are curved – the degree depends on where on the body the scute was situated – so before working, it may be necessary to flatten it. In order to change the shape of tortoiseshell in any way it must be heated. This can be done over fire, though as that risks burning it is normally heated in water to 80°C to which a little salt, oil or weak acid has been added. This process is also delicate, as too much heat causes the tortoiseshell to become opaque and polishing cannot turn it transparent again.

After it has been softened, the piece of tortoiseshell is placed between heated metal blocks with a lining of soft wood or bags of sand to absorb bumps in the surface that could otherwise cause the material to crack, and pressure or weight is put on the top block. The tortoiseshell is allowed to cool slowly in the press.

When flat, the scute can be filed down to the required thickness, care being taken to file it evenly. It is especially necessary to file away the rough surface of the underside of the scute, any deep scratches or any impurities left by barnacles.

The same process is pursued for bending the tortoiseshell as was used for flattening it: softening it first and then using heat and pressure. If it is to be shaped, two moulds are needed: one for the bottom and another in reverse shape to fit on top and push the tortoiseshell evenly on to the first mould. One mould will usually be concave in form and the other convex. For a small item, such as a bangle, the softened tortoiseshell is bent into the required shape by hand, by pressing it against a template.

When completely cool, the tortoiseshell will be as rigid as it was originally and will retain its new shape.

This method is also used for moulding patterns into tortoiseshell; for example, for mass-producing card cases instead of carving the pattern on each one individually (Fig. 45).

Fusing Tortoiseshell to Make Large Sheets or Thicker Sheets

To fuse tortoiseshell to make larger sheets, it must first be polished and then the edges to be fused must be filed down at an angle, so that when they overlap they are of the same thickness. It is necessary to ensure that they are scrupulously clean, with no trace of dust or even a fingerprint, as that will result in an unsuccessful join, which may later start to come apart.

The two edges to be joined are set over each other and held securely in place. It is not necessary to soften the tortoiseshell first. The pieces can be wrapped in wet cloth to provide the necessary moisture, put in a heated metal press and allowed to cool down there.

Fig. 53.
Handle of Neapolitan jug with piqué work, which has been formed by welding several layers of tortoiseshell before carving the shape of the handle. The layering is visible.

Fig. 54.
Tortoiseshell frog made by welding layers together before carving. The tortoiseshell is dark and the layers are not discernible. Made in Italy. Length about 4cm. ULLI FREYER

Fig. 55. Blond tortoiseshell box with gold piqué. Diameter 5.5cm.

Fig. 56. Tortoiseshell bangles. They have been bent into shape and the material welded with heat and pressure in a damp atmosphere to join up the circle.

Large, thin sheets of tortoiseshell were needed for veneer, both plain tortoiseshell veneer and also Boulle-style marquetry (*see* Marquetry and Boulle Style on page 95).

It is often possible to see where tortoiseshell has been joined because of the interruption in the pigmented pattern, though the actual join itself may not be visible. Masters of the craft can join pieces in such a way that the pattern aligns and there is no indication of the location of the join.

Thicker sheets are fused in the same way. Flat sheets are polished and cleaned, and are stacked on top of each other in a press.

They can be either softened first and immediately placed in the press while still wet, or wrapped in wet cloth.

Thick sheets of tortoiseshell were needed for items carved in relief, though some hawksbill scutes were sufficiently thick for low relief (Figs. 53 and 54). The blond plastron scutes of the hawksbill do not grow as thick as the carapacial scutes, so it was usually necessary to fuse sheets together in order to give a workable thickness for such items as dressing-table sets or boxes with piqué work (Fig. 55).

Making any items that were circular, such as cane handles or the sides of round boxes, necessitated fusing the tortoiseshell into rings (Fig. 56).

It should be noted that wild and farmed tortoiseshell reacts slightly differently to fusing treatments, so they cannot be used together.

Polishing

Tortoiseshell takes a high polish. It is accomplished by first scraping with an iron tool, then using sandpaper in various grades, finishing with a very fine one. Traditionally, the final polish is done with red lead powder or very fine pumice mixed with oil.

The oil must be chosen carefully, as some natural oils could go rancid and smell, while others could, with time, result in a cloudy film.

Today, polishing can be done in a less laborious way using with a metal polish, for example, chrome polish, and final polishing carried out on a buffing wheel with a very soft buff, at a gentle speed. Too much speed can generate too much heat, which can soften the tortoiseshell.

The tortoiseshell in objects with marquetry or piqué work were polished prior to mounting, as to polish them afterwards could result in the removal of a tiny amount of the surface of the tortoiseshell, which was the softer material. This could mean that the surface of the whole item was no longer completely smooth. A gentle polish was given to finish.

Piqué Work

Piqué work is the name given to decorating tortoiseshell with precious metals, usually gold and silver, which are inlaid into the material. There are two types: piqué posé and piqué point.

In piqué point, the pattern is formed by pressing tiny studs of metal into the material. Piqué posé uses strands of metal, or thin strips cut to resemble scrolls or patterns of some sort, pressed into the tortoiseshell to make a design or a picture (Fig. 57). At times, mother-of-pearl was used as well in piqué posé. Some of the finest work made in Europe in the early eighteenth century incorporated both styles.

▲ Fig. 57.
Glass jar with silver and tortoiseshell lid, made in England in the mid-twentieth century. The tortoiseshell has silver piqué pose. The jar was part of a dressing-table set.

The tiny studs, which could be of different sizes according to the desired pattern, were sometimes inserted into shallow incisions that acted as guidelines in the surface of the tortoiseshell, thus keeping patterns rigidly accurate. When the tortoiseshell was heated, the incisions disappeared as the material softened and the studs were pressed further in (Fig. 58).

Strips or strands of metal were very thin to allow them to be inserted into softened tortoiseshell without having first to remove any material. Thick pieces would dislodge too much of the material, resulting in an uneven surface. On the occasions where thicker material, such as mother-of-pearl, was used, the pattern had first to be incised in the tortoiseshell. On cooling, the tortoiseshell's own 'glue' held the pieces in place (Fig. 59).

All piqué work was done by hand until the late nineteenth century when a method was found of making it by machine. The styles became more geometric and rigid (*see also* Chapter 7).

Fig. 58. ▲
Tortoiseshell hair comb with gold piqué point. Probably made in France *c.* 1900.

Fig. 59.
Detail of the Neapolitan jug pictured in Fig. 88, showing the fine piqué work in silver, gold and etched mother-of-pearl.
GUILLAUME BENOIT

Marquetry and Boulle Style

Tortoiseshell has been used in different types of marquetry and veneer, sometimes with plain veneer covering the wood on the sides of a piece of furniture and marquetry on the front or the top. Marquetry was popular in Europe in the eighteenth and nineteenth centuries. On smaller items, such as musical instruments, it was often mixed with ivory and mother-of-pearl, rather than metals, the dark and light materials complementing one another in colour (Fig. 60).

Boulle style is the name given to intricate and extremely ornate tortoiseshell and brass or pewter marquetry on furniture, clocks and similar. It is named after André-Charles Boulle, although he did not himself start the style. He was especially famous for developing the *premier partie* and *contre partie* method of marquetry, where two identical pieces of furniture were covered in a form of negative and positive marquetry: *premier partie* with the pattern in metals on a background of tortoiseshell, and *contre partie* where it was the reverse: tortoiseshell pattern on a metal background.

Fig. 60.
Guitar with tortoiseshell and engraved ivory marquetry. Made in Germany in 1693 by Joachim Tielke. Body length 50cm. V&A MUSEUM

▲ Figs 61 and 62. ► A pair of toilet caskets made by André-Charles Boulle in the late 1680s. They were probably made for decorative purposes rather than utilitarian. Tortoiseshell and brass marquetry, with a little pewter, in the *premier partie* and *contre partie* style. Height of caskets on stands 138cm. RIJKSMUSEUM, AMSTERDAM

The precision required to make exact copies was accomplished by cutting both materials together, one on top of the other. When separated, it was possible to make up two complete sets of marquetry: one of each (Figs. 61 and 62).

In marquetry pieces of the various materials were glued first to a sheet of paper, forming the required pattern, before being attached to the wooden carcass of the furniture. In some cases, pigment was added; for example, in the dolls' house made for Petronella Oortmann, the tortoiseshell was backed with lead white, while Boulle sometimes used carbon black (Fig. 84).

The moulding on curved or carved surfaces was covered by hand with softened tortoiseshell and held in place with bags of sand that followed the contours. When it was cold and had retained its new shape, it could be glued in place.

The final polish was done with fine pumice and oil, or with carbon black and oil, the latter filling out any gaps between the tortoiseshell and the metal in the patterns.

The Boulle style of work remained popular until the late nineteenth century (*see* Chapter 7).

Backed Tortoiseshell, White, Gold, Red and Green

All natural tortoiseshell is coloured palest yellow through browns to almost black. There are no turtles with red or green scutes, and the 'green' name of one species alludes not to its scutes, but to the colour of its fat, which has a slightly greenish hue.

Because tortoiseshell is translucent in parts, it is possible to back it with paint or paper to give it the appearance of being coloured. It can also be backed with white to emphasize the mottled pattern or with gold foil to give it more lustre (Fig. 63).

The prepared and polished tortoiseshell is backed or painted before being attached as veneer to the surface of furniture or similar (Figs. 64 and 65).

'Red tortoiseshell' was popular in Holland in the seventeenth

Fig. 63.
Deconstructed dressing-table set of tortoiseshell with silver piqué. Note the coloured pigments used to back the brushes to enhance the colour in the tortoiseshell.

century and again in the nineteenth century. It was used a lot as veneer on cabinets, wall-mirror frames, bracket clocks and similar.

Tortoiseshell that is so dark that it resembles black lacquer may be loggerhead tortoiseshell backed with black, or it may be carefully chosen, very dark scutes from some hawksbills.

Dyed Tortoiseshell

Another way of altering the colour of tortoiseshell is by dyeing a thin layer of the material and sandwiching it between two thin layers of blond tortoiseshell. This is used today in Japan in the production of items such as spectacle frames or hair ornaments.

▲ Fig. 64.
Cabinet, made in Amsterdam in the mid-seventeenth century. Maker unknown. Tortoiseshell veneer on wood with bone stringing. The tortoiseshell has been backed with red pigment. Height of cabinet 150cm. RIJKSMUSEUM, AMSTERDAM

Fig. 65.
Sample of red-painted card overlaid with tortoiseshell to make the tortoiseshell appear red.

Glues

Pieces of tortoiseshell have the ability to fuse when treated with heat and pressure in a wet atmosphere, but there are occasions when glue has to be used; for example, when attaching it to a wooden surface.

A variety of glues has been recorded, all of them natural substances with no chemical additives. In Japan, egg albumin is recommended, while in other places, a glue made from boiling rabbit skins was preferred. Fish glue was not used for tortoiseshell as it tended to dry out in a matter of months.

It was also common to add pigment to the glue instead of using separate layers of glue and paint in order to obtain the effect of colour or to emphasize the mottling in the tortoiseshell.

Bekko Wor

Bekko is the Japanese word for tortoiseshell from the hawksbill turtle. The art of working with bekko has long been a custom in Japan, and the craftsmen there have, without doubt, taken the work to a very high level. There are still bekko artists in Japan, though today there are far fewer than before. The art cannot

Fig. 66.
Japanese bekko work box. The body of the box is moulded mottled tortoiseshell with no wooden carcass, and with a blond tortoiseshell dragon inset. Length of box 10cm. ULLI FREYER

survive without a supply of tortoiseshell. There is talk of farming hawksbills in the south of the country, but it will take a long time for the turtles to reach a sufficient size to be able to harvest their shells.

Only hawksbill tortoiseshell is used in Japan, as both wild green and farmed green have been found lacking. The artists work in the same way and using the same type of tools today as has been done for 400 years, with the possible exception of polishing at the end of the process, which is now done on a buffing wheel rather than laboriously by hand with a soft leather or leaves.

The first step is choosing the right scute and deciding how to use the mottled pattern to best advantage. A design is drawn on the scute and sawn out using a small bow saw, and is then filed to the required thickness. If a thicker piece is needed, several pieces may be cut out the same shape and tied together before being fused in hot water and a press.

With more heat and steam, the material can be softened again and formed either by gentle bending or by moulding. The fused pieces do not come apart.

Blond tortoiseshell from the animal's plastron has always been popular with bekko craftsmen, as have the very dark mottled scutes. They could be used to make designs or patterns, sometimes being joined together to form stripes or pictures. The pattern in the mottling in the carapacial scutes has also been skilfully utilized as part of the final design, which necessitated great care in joining pieces together. The fact that tortoiseshell is thermoplastic and becomes rigid when once formed, has also meant that three-dimensional sculptures were possible, in many cases without a wooden carcass (Fig. 66).

▲ Fig. 67.
Tortoiseshell dish, with lacquer decoration. Made in Japan for the Western market in the Meiji period. Decorative purposes only, not utilitarian. The dish is damaged and missing part of the lip. Width 28.5cm.

Today, the items made are mostly plain hair adornments or spectacle frames, but in years past, ornate objects were made, such as small boxes, dishes or combs, which were decorated with lacquer. Sometimes extra materials were added as part of the decoration; for example, coral or mother-of-pearl, and gold powder or foil. The lacquer used came from the sap of the *Urushi* tree and was very toxic. On tortoiseshell it was normally used without pigment, though some decorations called for areas to be lacquered with pigment as well. Many of the pigments were also extremely toxic.

A popular form of lacquer work on tortoiseshell was maki-e, which involved painting a picture in clear lacquer on the surface and, while it was wet, sprinkling it with gold powder to form a design (Fig. 67).

Care of Tortoiseshell

Tortoiseshell is inert to water and to very weak acid, and also to many solvents, though there are some that contain chemicals that can cause damage.

Tortoiseshell is susceptible to damage from UV light, dust, a damp atmosphere or too much heat. The surface can go dull and matt, and the growth lines of the scutes reappear as a faint pattern of wavy lines. The result is easily seen on a tortoiseshell item such as a box that has become dull on the outside, while the inside retains its high polish because it is more protected.

Tortoiseshell is mildly hygroscopic, that is, it can absorb moisture, and it can also dry out. This happens if it gets too hot, as in a lit display case or a sunny windowsill, or if it is placed on a mantelpiece or near a radiator. The result can be warping, flaking or cracking. Equally, it should not be kept in a damp atmosphere as that can cause the surface to go dull and uneven.

It is possible to clean tortoiseshell using a slightly moist, very soft cloth. Care must be taken not to make it wet, and not to dislodge inlay or damage carving. It is not a suitable method to use on tortoiseshell marquetry.

When it becomes dull, it must be re-polished to bring it back to its beautiful, shiny state. This cannot be achieved with household polishes or with oils, and each time it is re-polished with abrasives a small amount of the surface is ground away. It is advisable to seek professional help if any item needs to be cleaned or re-polished.

Polishing piqué work or marquetry should be avoided, if possible, as it can result in an uneven surface, where the harder metal areas become raised above the softer tortoiseshell. Also, it is very easy to catch the edge of the metal and dislodge it during polishing (Fig. 68).

Tortoiseshell, like all keratins, is susceptible to damage by insects, especially clothes' moth lavae, which gnaw small areas,

▲ Fig. 68.
Damaged mirror back. The tortoiseshell has warped badly and some piqué is missing.

usually around the edge of an item. Care should, therefore, be taken not to risk a moth infestation where tortoiseshell artefacts are stored (Fig. 69).

When tortoiseshell items need repair it is unlikely that it will be possible to replace missing material, due to the strict laws protecting marine turtles. There are few restorers who have stockpiles of raw tortoiseshell that they can use, and laws often forbid its use anyhow. Some museums no longer use tortoiseshell for repairs, either for ethical reasons or because of a lack of the raw material. In other cases the museum believes that an item should be brought back to as near its original state as possible, and if they are in possession of any raw tortoiseshell, and local laws permit, they will use it. Tortoiseshell remains thermoplastic and, if it has been kept in suitable conditions, can still be worked even when it is many years old.

Note: Horn should be cared for in the same way as tortoiseshell.

Fig. 69.
Tortoiseshell damaged by insects, probably clothes moths larvae, which have eaten parts of the material making it appear chipped.

Care of Plastic Imitations

Plastics can be cleaned by gentle washing, but care should be taken not to make an item too wet, especially if it has any metal fittings.

Plastics are not hard materials and can easily be scratched. Some can also warp or their colours fade if left in sunlight.

It is unknown how long synthetic and semi-synthetic polymers will last, but so far it seems that natural polymers are more durable. It may be that the newest plastics will last a long time, but museums have very real problems with the storage of plastics, because when they start to degrade, nothing can be done to halt or reverse the process and they need to be isolated.

Plastics should never be stored in airtight containers but should be loosely wrapped separately in acid-free paper and stored in a ventilated environment.

Early plastics with metal mounts, pins or hinges are particularly susceptible to the problem. The first sign of trouble is usually that the area around the metal starts to go green (Fig. 70).

The warning signs of imminent degrading are warping, discoloration, surface crazing, blisters and the fumes typical of each plastic: thus celluloid will smell of camphor, cellulose acetate of vinegar, and so forth.

At the first indication of any of the above, the item should be separated from any other items, especially plastic ones, as the chemicals given off can cause damage or even trigger the process in another item (Fig. 71).

◄ Fig. 70.
Detail of celluloid glove stretchers, which have degraded and are falling to pieces. Note the green discoloration around the metal hinge, which hastens the damage.

Fig. 71.▲
Imitation tortoiseshell candlestick, the shaft is of casein but the base is possibly cellulose acetate. The mottling is unconvincing, especially on the shaft.

Chapter 7

History

Introduction

Turtles, tortoises and terrapins (freshwater turtles) belong to the taxonomic order Testudines. What is commonly referred to as tortoiseshell comes from three species of marine turtle only, primarily hawksbill turtles. Green turtles and, to a lesser extent, loggerhead turtles have also been used occasionally for tortoiseshell.

Testudines have featured in many cultures world-wide, and for many millennia. Ancient writings do not distinguish between the various types and, indeed, in many languages today the same word is used for all of them. It is difficult, therefore, to know exactly to what is being referred in the old texts, and some guesswork is involved. Many ancient beliefs and myths covered all of them.

The keratinous scutes of marine turtles are in English called by the misnomer 'tortoiseshell'. The material derives from marine turtles, not from tortoises, and the name is due to an early misconception when turtles were referred to as sea tortoises by early naturalists. Nonetheless, tortoiseshell is the accepted term for the material and, as such, is not confused with other parts of the animal's shell. Tortoiseshell is not durable and degrades with time, so this, too, can complicate matters when trying to understand the history behind it: how it was used, when and where. There is little tortoiseshell still in existence that is as much as 500 years old.

This chapter gives examples of many of the uses of turtles through the ages in various parts of the world. It in no way condones the use of parts of the animals purely for decoration, but endeavours to explain humankind's fascination with them, and the uses to which they have been put.

Ancient Times

In various countries in the Middle East, turtle remains have been found in middens and in ancient burial mounds and chambers dating back 5,000 years. Whether the animals were symbolic or, in some instances, simply food, is not easy to establish. Those found in the burial chambers of people who were obviously of high rank were possibly psychopomps – there to guide the person on his or her way to the next world, or the animals may have been sacrificed as part of the funerary rituals, as is thought to be the case in Eastern Arabia where green turtles were used in funerary ceremonies from about 4,000BC. There was also a belief that turtle bones were apotropaic and guarded against evil. This belief continues in parts of Anatolia even today and bones may be seen hanging in houses or beside a child's cradle to ward off evil.

In the old burial sites it is usually not possible to know exactly which species of turtle or tortoise has been found, and assumptions are made that the remains are those of local fauna. For example, skeletons of turtles found in burial sites in Turkey, which date from somewhere between 700 and 400BC, would appear to be mostly from the Euphrates soft-shelled turtle (a type of freshwater turtle) and are thought to have been part of a funerary ritual, as they show signs of having been butchered.

Tortoiseshell has been traded in the Middle East for a very long time. In about 2400BC boats were already sailing from what is today India, up the Persian Gulf to the Akkadian Empire (later part of Mesopotamia). By the end of the third millennium BC there were trade routes though much of Mesopotamia, carrying items such as timber, grain, cloth, ivory, copper and tin. Luxury articles, such as pearls, coral and tortoiseshell, were carried to the Babylonian markets from Dilmun – the area along the west coast of the Persian Gulf in what is today Saudi Arabia.

Large amounts of turtle remains have been found in Dilmun. Turtles were actively hunted and were fished in the sea, where they were foraging in coral reefs, and females were taken when nesting. It is likely that their eggs were also consumed. Judging by the marks on many of the bones found, the animals were butchered, indicating that they were hunted for food.

At its zenith, the Babylonian Empire (1984–539BC) stretched from the Mediterranean to the Red Sea and the Persian Gulf, so the Babylonians had plenty of access to turtles, yet it seems that they imported them from Dilmun as well as catching them themselves. Old cuneiform texts inform us that in Babylonia the turtles were roasted to preserve their meat, and other written accounts tell that the Babylonians had skilled craftsmen who were able to use tortoiseshell to decorate furniture and make jewellery, such as rings, commissioned by people of very high rank. It has been concluded that the turtles taken as food by the Babylonians were probably freshwater turtles from the Euphrates and the Tigris Rivers. These turtles do not produce tortoiseshell, so the material for decorative purposes came from Dilmun as trade goods.

In Ancient Egypt, turtles were represented in hieroglyphs and the paintings in burial chambers. Tortoiseshell was used for items such as knife handles, combs, bracelets and amulets in the Middle Kingdom (about 2050–1710BC). The source was probably hawksbills from the Red Sea. It is said that Queen Hatshepsut (1508–1458BC) sent a trading expedition to the fabled land of Punt near the southern end of the Red Sea, which returned with gold, ivory, live animals, trees and tortoiseshell. It had been many centuries since anyone had traded there and the expedition was a great success.

There is evidence that turtles were served as food, but that was more likely to have been freshwater turtles from the Nile than marine turtles.

An Egyptian compilation of medical texts dated about 1550BC called *Ebers Papyrus* is one of the oldest known medical works. It contains hundreds of formulae and spells for cures, giving advice on a broad spectrum of problems ranging from snake bites to how to rid a house of pests such as rats. Some of the remedies mention turtle carapaces and organs.

Ancient Greece and Rome

Our knowledge of the use of tortoiseshell in Ancient Greece is somewhat limited, but the Greeks were traders as far back as the Bronze Age, so it is likely that tortoiseshell was one of the luxury goods, often imported along with ivory and pearls. Indeed, an old Greek text from the second century AD lists a shipment coming from East Africa that included lots of ivory, plus rhinoceros horn and tortoiseshell. There is evidence of a musical instrument using turtle shell, but it was the bones rather than the scutes that were used, though the instrument could conceivably have still been covered by keratin. A whole turtle or tortoise carapace formed the body of the stringed musical instrument called a chelys lyre. According to Greek mythology the chelys was invented by Hermes.

More is known about the Ancient Romans' use of tortoiseshell, as it became extremely fashionable in the last century BC and first century AD. During the last century, Julius Caesar is said to have had warehouses full of tortoiseshell taken as war booty in his Egyptian conquests, though large amounts were being imported along with ivory to satisfy the demands of the Roman elite who were keen to adorn their homes with such exotic items. Plutarch wrote that the homes were lavishly decorated purely to impress visitors, while Propertius and Horace both wrote that they would not have such items in their homes, as their reputations were not dependent upon such excesses. They were not alone in their condemnation. Pliny the Elder also complained about the indulgence, which he did not think enhanced any feast.

From Pliny we have a description of how the tortoiseshell was imported, and how it was worked in AD50. Large amounts of turtles were fished in the Azanian Sea (off the coast of today's Eritrea) and their tortoiseshell exported from a port called Adulis, together with ivory, rhino horn, hippopotamus hides, apes and slaves, brought from the interior by Africans. The tortoiseshell was sent to the Roman Empire, where it was cut into panels and polished, and used to decorate expensive furniture.

Occasionally the tortoiseshell was dyed in order to enhance it or to make it resemble certain exotic and expensive woods, even though its value was already very high, being two-thirds of that of ivory.

Tables, chairs, eight-seater couches, beds, cradles, doorframes and doors were all veneered in tortoiseshell, ivory and mother-of-pearl. There was even mention in one text of a solid ivory bedstead that was inlaid with tortoiseshell. These lavish pieces could be bought in the bazaars and, in some cases, the contents of a home were thought to be worth more than the building itself. All were guarded vigilantly by slaves.

Different types of tortoiseshell were imported from different countries, and it was claimed that the best tortoiseshell came from Golden Island off the Indian east coast. The next best was sent from Rhapta, a port managed by Arabs on the north-east coast of Africa. On the other hand, the ivory from there was considered inferior to that from Adulis.

The *Periplus Maris Erythraea*, written in the first century AD, tells of the goods' trades and the routes taken in the Erythraean Sea (the name given then to the seas and gulfs from Africa to India). It confirms that tortoiseshell was by then traded from the east coast of Africa, Arabia and India, the routes going back and forth, voyages undertaken at certain times of the year and dependent upon the winds to carry the ships down the Red Sea from the trading ports, and the monsoons to carry them to Arabia and across to India. Tortoiseshell was just one of many items that would have been on board for trade. Ivory was also often on the list, taken from elephants north of the Sahara before they became extinct there.

Other things included Egyptian cloth, Indian cotton, silks, spices, sometimes slaves and beautiful ladies for a king for concubinage. Wine was also carried, though not always for sale. It was taken to 'entertain the barbarians' (anyone who did not speak Latin or live in the Roman Empire), to make them more compliant.

China

In Ancient China, turtle plastrons (or ox scapula) were used as oracle bones. Various remains have been found dating from about 1600–1050BC. Diviners asked questions of the deities by carving them into the bones, which were then heated until the bone cracked. In later examples, the questions were painted on using cinnabar – a toxic, red pigment made from mercury. The

Fig. 72.
Two carved boxes, produced in China for the Western market, probably mid-nineteenth century. Diameter of larger box, 10cm.

Fig. 73.
Detail of the top of the larger box in Fig.72. The carving is in high relief, although the tortoiseshell has not been welded. This is possible because of the thickness of the hawksbill turtle's scutes.

way in which the bone cracked was interpreted by the diviner, to provide answers to the questions. The carved bones are the earliest examples of Chinese writing.

Throughout Asia, turtles were regarded as totally reliable and steadfast creatures. They move slowly and never hurry, which signified wisdom and patience. Because they live to a good age, they were also regarded as a symbol of longevity. This symbolism is illustrated by some of the memorial tablets erected in China in the Sui Dynasty (AD58–618) and again in the Ming Dynasty (AD1368–1644), which stand on carved stone turtles. Legend says that the Hall of Supreme Harmony in the Forbidden City in Beijing (built between AD1406 and AD1420) is built upon the backs of live turtles.

From about 2500BC until 220BC tortoiseshell was used as currency in China, supplementing the more usual cowrie shell currency. The cowrie shells were for smaller transactions, the tortoiseshell for larger ones, but it is not possible to deduce whether the material in question was the scutes of marine turtles or a tortoise shell, meaning a land-based tortoise carapace.

The earliest mention of worked tortoiseshell in China was made by Confucius (551–479BC). After that, little is known until records state that Dutch traders brought tortoiseshell to the country in the early nineteenth century, where it was used to make hair ornaments and other small items. Soon China was producing boxes and other objects for the Western market. Among them were small, round boxes entirely covered in decoration, the tops carved in deeper relief than the base. They usually depicted Chinese scenes (Figs. 72 and 73).

An exception was the decorative snuff bottles, which are today collectors' items but were made in China for the Chinese market. Smoking tobacco was forbidden at one stage during the Qing Dynasty, so it became the custom to powder the tobacco and use it as snuff instead. Little bottles with stoppers were made of delicately painted porcelain or other materials, such as amber and rhino horn. In later years they were also made of intricately carved tortoiseshell, and today they are being 'faked' in plastic (Fig. 43).

India and Ceylon

In the Hindu faith, a turtle was the second incarnation of Vishnu. It is not clear whether there was a belief in that faith that turtles were synonymous with long life. From records it would appear that India's role in the tortoiseshell market was very much one of trade, both in raw scutes and in finished goods for export, though early European travellers to India recorded items of furniture inlaid with ivory, tortoiseshell, mother-of-pearl and metal wire.

In India, tortoiseshell was treated over the centuries mostly as a veneer. The beautiful caskets made in Gujarat in the sixteenth and seventeenth centuries for the Portuguese market were more of an exception than the norm. Made of mottled or blond tortoiseshell with silver fittings and corners, they were sent back to Portugal for personal use by the wealthy or for use in churches to serve as reliquaries or ciboria (Fig. 74).

Fig. 74.
Blond tortoiseshell casket with silver mounts. No wooden frame or carcass. Made in India for the Portuguese in the late sixteenth to early seventeenth century. Width 26cm. V&A MUSEUM

Fig. 75.
Wooden box covered in tortoiseshell with ivory fretwork and other decoration. Typical of the work produced in Vizagapatam in the nineteenth century, for Western settlers or the Western market.

The Indo-British tortoiseshell and ivory items made in Vizagapatam in the nineteenth century are much more typical of Indian work. There tortoiseshell was used as a veneer on a sandalwood base and overlaid with etched ivory panels or carved fretwork. Buffalo and bison horn or porcupine quills could be used instead of tortoiseshell and bone, substituted for ivory on less expensive pieces. Large items, such as chess tables, and boxes in all sizes were popular, used for storing gloves, handkerchiefs, jewellery, sewing articles, work tools and so forth (Fig. 75).

Ceilao, as it was called under Portuguese governance, later Ceylon and now Sri Lanka, was one of the countries that exported large amounts of both raw scutes and such finished objects as cigar boxes and combs. Green turtles were butchered for food. The animals were treated cruelly – as they were in most places – and in the late-nineteenth century laws were brought in to prevent the cruelty, instigated by the Humane Society in England. As was the custom world-wide, females were taken on the beaches after egg-laying and before they could return to the sea. They were then bound and held upside down over a fire till the scutes fell off the carapace, after which they were freed to return to the sea, as it was thought that their keratinous layer would regrow. Although the keratin does keep growing, it was highly unlikely that any animal could survive the ordeal or survive in the sea without the protective layer on its shell. The reason for the barbaric treatment of the turtles was that it was believed that the scutes had to be removed from a living turtle in order to prevent them becoming cloudy. Such was the demand for turtles in Sri Lanka that they were also imported from India.

The Ottoman Empire

Some of the oldest remaining examples of tortoiseshell date from during the Ottoman Empire. The magnificent throne of Ahmed I (1603–17), made during his reign and which can be seen at the Topkapi Museum in Istanbul, is one such example.

It is a single-seat throne with a baldachin, the throne made of lacquered wood inlaid with mother-of-pearl and tortoiseshell, set with precious gems.

Islamic decoration tends to be of geometric or animal and vegetal design, the latter keeping a somewhat regular pattern rather being completely free flowing. Geometric marquetry consisting of different woods in diamond or triangular shapes, often with the addition of mother-of-pearl and sometimes with tortoiseshell, featured on chairs, stools, tables and boxes. Where floral designs were used, the tortoiseshell and mother-of-pearl were inlaid on wood using the intarsia technique, each piece being precisely cut and applied separately. Examples in remarkably good condition, and thought to date from the late-sixteenth century, have occasionally appeared at auction.

Tortoiseshell was used for some small items, for example, spoons, which were an important part of life in the Ottoman Empire. Food was mostly eaten using the hands or with a spoon, and spoon-making was a recognized craft. The spoon-makers in Istanbul made valuable spoons for the Ottoman elite using a combination of materials, such as ivory, horn, tortoiseshell, coral and mother-of-pearl. Tortoiseshell – unlike metals – has no flavour and was, therefore, ideal. The shape of the bowl of the spoon dictated its use. The spoons traditionally used for sweet items, such as compotes, had hemispherical bowls and straight, slim handles. Today they are commonly referred to as

▲ Fig. 76.
Two Turkish sherbet spoons. The handles are bone and the almost hemispherical bowls are tortoiseshell. Early nineteenth century. Length 25cm.

sherbet spoons, from the Arabic word *sharbât*, although sherbets are, in fact, drinks made from fruit and spices sweetened with sugar or honey (Fig. 76).

Polynesia

Throughout history, turtles have been used as food. Marine turtles have been consumed by people living in the coastal areas of almost all countries with a tropical or sub-tropical climate, especially where the turtles were plentiful. The animals could be caught by harpooning or in nets in the water, both of which required some skill. By contrast, it was easy to catch female turtles when they came ashore to lay their eggs, as they move slowly on land and could be completely immobilized by flipping them on to their backs. Turtle meat and eggs provided valuable, free protein. Until the turtle bans came in about fifty years ago, many communities had relied upon the availability of turtles to survive; indeed, with the bans came malnourishment and near-starvation in some poor communities. In many places the decorative, keratinous part of the shells of the turtles was merely a by-product and was often thrown away.

An exception to the diet of turtle meat was the islands of the South Pacific, especially Polynesia, where turtles were plentiful but were consumed only by the elite on special occasions, as they were considered sacred.

The Polynesian people were seafarers, with their origins somewhere in Asia – possibly Taiwan – about 5,000–6,000 years ago. They share this heritage with most of the Pacific islanders. They belonged to the Lapita Culture, and over the centuries they discovered and inhabited the Pacific Islands from Hawaii in the north to Rapa Nui (Easter Island) in the east and, finally, in about AD1200–1350, they discovered Aotearoa (New Zealand). It is now believed that their navigation across the vast expanses of ocean relied not only on the sun, moon and stars, plus ocean currents and winds, but also on turtles. Swimming at a depth of about one metre, a turtle would have travelled at approximately the same average speed as the sailing canoes.

As they shared the same culture, the inhabitants of the various islands were in many ways similar and held the same beliefs and maintained the same customs and language. Being such adept sailors, they also traded with each other, sailing hundreds of kilometres between the islands. Sadly, our knowledge of their history is scant and at times contradictory, because it relies on the early writings of the first Western explorers to visit the islands in the nineteenth century. As the Western explorers prohibited the traditional practices of the islanders and converted them to Christianity, we are left guessing at much of their past.

It seems obvious that turtles held a special place in their customs. It is known that in the Marquesas Islands turtles were used as funerary sacrifices. When human sacrifices were banned, turtles were sacrificed instead.

Throughout Polynesia, turtle meat was eaten only by the chiefs or priests at certain ceremonies, though there is mention that in some places when those dignitaries had had their fill, men and boys from the community were allowed to eat the scraps – but it was forbidden for women to partake.

In later years, the sacred status of the turtle diminished, and by the time the fishing bans had come into force, all the islanders had begun to eat the animals.

Body ornaments and jewellery were similar across many of the Pacific Islands. Jewellery was worn every day and extra lavishly for ceremonies. It was precious to them, as it was possibly their only possession. Some individuals were buried with their jewellery, while in other instances, items were passed down and became heirlooms, their power being extra strong because of the connection to the ancestors.

Jewellery was made by craftsmen, and they are renowned for having had the ability to use every form of organic gem material available; for example, many types of shell, whale ivory, porpoise and dogs' teeth, boars' tusks, various seeds, animal fur, human hair, feathers and tortoiseshell. All jewellery had a symbolism that was understood and could thus communicate unique meanings.

Tortoiseshell jewellery was generally worn on or around the head, which may have had some further symbolism as the head was sacrosanct and not allowed to be touched. Nose ornaments and ear ornaments were cut from flat pieces of tortoiseshell, the former worn by boys who had had their septa cut to allow the ornament to be inserted. Tortoiseshell pendants in the shape of fishhooks were the domain of women.

Kapkaps were worn by men on the forehead on bands of woven fibres or as a pendant on a string around the neck (Fig. 77). Thin pieces of tortoiseshell were skilfully cut into intricate patterns of

Fig. 77.
Kapkap of giant clam shell overlaid with finely carved tortoiseshell fretwork. They were used in several of the Polynesian islands, worn either as a pendant or on a band around the head. THE AUCKLAND WAR MEMORIAL MUSEUM, NEW ZEALAND

geometric and anthropomorphic design and placed over a round slice of Tridacna or giant clam shell. Until metal tools became available, the cutting was done using a shark's tooth. Similar discs were used as pendants for men to wear on the breast at important ceremonies or when going to war. These *tema* discs were larger than those used for *kapkaps*, and the tortoiseshell pattern on top was a simple representation of a frigate bird and much less intricate.

One of the most striking uses of tortoiseshell was as a crown or *pa'e kaha* worn by men or women of rank in the Marquesas Islands and, apparently, the custom was that they were paid for with pigs. Here, alternate curved plates of incised tortoiseshell and triton shell were held together on a woven, fibre band, at the ends of which were plates of shell with an overlay of tortoiseshell fretwork (Fig. 78). So impressive were they that, in later years, some very convincing fakes were made in early plastics and sold to unsuspecting collectors and tourists. It has even been suggested that one or two found their way into museum collections.

Fig. 78.
Pa'e kaha or crown from the Marquesas Islands. Made from giant clam shell and tortoiseshell. The tortoiseshell is incised with patterns. THE TRUSTEES OF THE BRITISH MUSEUM

New Zealand and Australia

Although discovered and settled by people from the Eastern Polynesian islands, New Zealand has developed differently. The Maori settlers and their customs became very much their own, as did their decorative habits. Much of the country lies in a cooler latitude, so there are fewer marine turtles than around the more northern Pacific Islands. Greens and loggerheads can be seen around the northernmost part of New Zealand, but hawksbills very rarely visit; therefore, turtles did not feature much in Maori culture, and tortoiseshell was hardly used. A 600-year-old canoe was found a few years ago, washed up on a beach on a north-west coast of South Island after a storm. On the hull was a clear carving of a turtle, and it is thought that it was somehow connected to the other Polynesian islands, although the wood was local.

In contrast to New Zealand, six species of marine turtle are found around Australia, mostly on the northern coasts. Further, there is one marine turtle species that is only found around Australia, the flatback (*Natator depressus*).

Hawksbill, green and loggerheads all nest in Australia, especially in the Indo-Pacific region, and although hunting them is generally banned in the country, they may be legally hunted by Aboriginal and Torres Strait Islander people for 'personal, domestic or non-commercial communal needs'.

Turtles have always had important cultural and social worth for Aboriginals and Torres Straits islanders, and they have often featured in Aboriginal cave paintings and in the Dreamtime stories. They have occupied important roles in ceremonies, and their meat and eggs provide valuable and nutritious food. After slaughtering, the animals could be slow cooked in their shells, which, of course, destroyed the keratinous tortoiseshell layer; but tortoiseshell was not, generally, of much interest to the local people and its use was limited.

The uses and symbolism of many Aboriginal artefacts is not fully understood and, besides, can be a closely guarded secret. Today, it is still not allowed to make images of any cultural property without first gaining permission. Some of the things made from tortoiseshell have been painted, but the symbolism is not known.

One of the most common uses for the tortoiseshell was as fish-hooks. The material could be cut and then bent into shape by heating a rounded pebble in a fire and then pressing the tortoise-shell against it. The point was sharpened and the hook attached to a mother-of-pearl shaft, which could catch the light in the water and act as a lure. A few other items have been found in cave shrines, such as a figure of a bird made of plates of tortoiseshell sewn together with twine. Tortoiseshell was also used occasionally as adornment; for example, as plain, narrow bangles and as breast ornaments combined with seashells. The material had a few utilitarian uses too, such as filing one edge of a scute till it was sharp and could be used as a cutting implement.

The Torres Straits islanders were adept at fashioning tortoise-shell and are renowned for their tortoiseshell funerary masks. The simpler styles depicted a human face and were often painted in red, yellow and blue. Some were adorned with human hair. A more complex style was a large mask, commonly incorporating haliotis and other shells, plus cassowary feathers. The cassowary is a large and rather fierce bird, so its feathers gave extra power to the wearer of the mask and evinced awe in its beholder. The pieces of tortoiseshell were bound or sewn together with twine. The mask was worn over the head rather than covering just the face, and usually depicted both a human face and an animal such as a frigate bird or a fish (Fig. 79). A lot of work went into making the masks, and the tortoiseshell was often embossed with a pattern, for example, denoting the feathers on the frigate bird's wings. The masks were full of symbolism and could only be worn by spiritual leaders of high rank who could communicate with the ancestors. As with the crowns of the Marquesas Islands, the funerary masks of the Torres Straits have been copied in plastic and sold as tourist souvenirs.

A dark chapter in the area's history is the so-called Ngatik massacre. In 1836, an Australian trading cutter was in search of tortoiseshell and pearl shells. By this time tortoiseshell was fetching exceedingly high prices in Europe and Japan. The captain

Fig. 79. ▲
Ceremonial mask from the Islands of the Torres Straits depicting a head and a frigate bird. Made from tortoiseshell, with haliotis shells and cassowary feathers. The tortoiseshell on the bird's wings is incised with lines to represent feathers. Nineteenth century. NATIONAL MUSEUMS OF SCOTLAND

believed that there was a stockpile of tortoiseshell on the island of Sapwuahfik in Micronesia, but his attempts at capturing it were rebuffed. Returning the next year he massacred most of the islanders, only to discover that the stock of tortoiseshell was nowhere near the value he had anticipated.

Mesoamerica and the Caribbean, and the Early Discoverers

Across the Pacific Ocean in Mesoamerica, turtles were of great importance and featured in Ancient Mayan culture, where they were considered to have religious, symbolic and cosmological importance. In one legend, the sun turned into a turtle in order to avoid being drowned by a thunderbolt from the rain god, Chaac.

Another legend tells that Chaac was present at the resurrection of a Mayan maize god from the carapace of a turtle, which possibly represented the earth.

From remains found it is reasonable to assume that turtles were consumed by local populations. It is known that tortoiseshell was esteemed and utilized, though only one item exists containing tortoiseshell. It is one of the oldest identifiable remnants of tortoiseshell that exists (if not the oldest) and is a small square on a pre-Hispanic mosaic mask. The mask, which is in the collections at Dumbarton Oaks in Washington DC, has a wooden base, turquoise mosaic, a face with protruding teeth resembling fangs and wooden squares denoting earlobe ornaments, one of which is covered with degraded tortoiseshell. The mask is dated to between AD1200 and AD1520.

Although some tortoiseshell was used for jewellery and instruments, turtles featured first and foremost as food around Central America and the Caribbean Islands – until the arrival of Europeans at the end of the fifteenth century.

Local populations relied on turtle meat and eggs, and the Europeans were quick to realize that turtles could provide a valuable source of fresh protein on their long journeys. Ships' logs record that, in those days, there were so many turtles that Christopher Columbus said they were banging against his ship and clogging the entrance to a harbour in the Bahamas in 1492, and that they made so much noise that his men complained they were kept awake at night. The Spanish explorer and conquistador, Ponce de León, who led the first official European expedition to Florida, captured 170 nesting turtles from the nearby islands in 1513 to take on one of his voyages. Generally, the turtles were caught by locals for sale to the explorers to be stored on board ship for slaughter during the voyage. Sometimes the sailors endeavoured to catch the animals themselves but, although it was easy to immobilize a turtle by 'turning' it, the task was not without some danger as the turtles could give a very nasty bite that could take off a few fingers. Once on board ship, they were kept immobile by being laid on their backs and watered down from time to time. In this way they could be kept alive for extended periods of time. Over the next centuries it became the custom for trading ships to stock up with turtles for the journey, stopping at certain locations, such as Ascension Island in the mid-Atlantic, where the animals were abundant. Turtles were harvested on Ascension Island for over 200 years, with the result that the turtle population was totally decimated and new sources had to be found. It was believed that not only did the turtles provide food, but that they had therapeutic properties, having the ability to cure pre-existing diseases. The custom of stocking up with turtles was not confined to the Caribbean and the Atlantic: in the mid-eighteenth century, the British explorer Captain James Cook provisioned his ships with turtles on his voyages of discovery around the Pacific Ocean and Oceania.

In some instances, turtles were carried from the Caribbean back to England with the idea of selling the fresh meat there, as it was regarded as a great and exotic delicacy. Unsurprisingly, most of them did not survive the long trip. Records show that on one occasion only one out of sixty turtles was still alive by the time the ship reached England. Nevertheless, turtles were so abundant at that time that even slaves on the ships were fed some of the meat in an effort to stop them succumbing to illness and dying on the way to the slave markets.

Following the colonization of parts of Central America and the West Indies by the Spanish in the sixteenth century, tortoiseshell, known locally as *carey*, began to be exported to Europe. The material was not unknown in Europe, even though its use by Ancient civilizations was long forgotten. There were turtles in the Mediterranean, and tortoiseshell was imported from the East Indies and the coasts of Africa and Arabia. Yet it seems that little was used for decorative purposes in Europe before it began to arrive from the West Indies. Indeed, in France turtles had, until then, been considered more of medicinal use than anything else.

As well as raw tortoiseshell being sent to Spain, the Mayan people manufactured many objects from tortoiseshell specifically for the Spanish market. These included boxes, fans, combs such as the famous Spanish *peinetas* worn by women to secure their *mantillas* or lace head coverings, jewellery, and *chiqueadores* or

Fig. 80.
Tortoiseshell *peineta*, made to be worn under a *mantilla*. Probably made in Chile in the mid-nineteenth century. V&A MUSEUM

beauty spots, which women attached to their faces, sometimes using two or three at a time. Sacred items were also produced embellished with tortoiseshell. In 1648, a large tortoiseshell cross was sent to Seville for use in the Holy Week processions. Naturally, the new inhabitants of the Spanish colonies also wished to possess the costly material and had taken their customs with them, so, for example, the Spanish fashion of wearing a *mantilla* and a *peineta* soon became the fashion for many South American ladies and is a custom that survives today (Fig. 80).

It was not only Spain that was conquering foreign lands. Portugal had one of the biggest empires in the world, which it started in 1415 when the first explorers set out. It was a Portuguese explorer, Vasco da Gama, who was the first European to reach India by sea after sailing round the southern tip of Africa. Until then, any trade had been conducted partly by ship and partly overland. So successful were the Spanish and Portuguese at colonization, that in 1494 an agreement called the Treaty of Tordesillas was reached, which basically divided the world between them, roughly giving the Western Hemisphere to Spain and the Eastern Hemisphere to Portugal, though Portugal retained the largest country of all – Brazil – in the Western Hemisphere.

Many of Portugal's colonies had access to marine turtles, but tortoiseshell was not sent back to Europe from Asia. Instead it was traded around the Asian countries where it was in demand, and worked items were sent home to Portugal; for example, the previously mentioned tortoiseshell caskets dating from the sixteenth and seventeenth centuries that were made in India (Figs. 81, 74).

After many battles and various treaties, by the eighteenth century, France and Britain had taken over control of most of the region around the Caribbean and Central America. The production of tortoiseshell items being made in Spain was reduced, but with control of the tortoiseshell trade, France became the centre for tortoiseshell craftsmanship.

Fig. 81. ▲
Indo-Portuguese casket of blond tortoiseshell and silver fittings. Note the absence of any carcass or frame. Sixteenth century. Length 21cm. Santa Casa da Misericórdia de Lisboa/Museu de São Roque, inv. Rl. 1041. CINTRA & CASTRO CALDAS, LDA

As well as tortoiseshell from hawksbill turtles, green and loggerhead scutes were sent to Europe. Records show that they were taxed at about half of the tax levied on the hawksbill material, though the tax payable on them was still higher than that charged for slaves.

Madacascar

In another part of the world, Madagascar was populated by many different nationalities and cultures over the centuries, starting with people from the Malay Archipelago about 2,000 years ago, and by the nineteenth century, the British and French were each trying to claim it for their own. Long before that it had become famous as a source of hawksbill tortoiseshell. According to early records, it was already an important export by AD1613, and the export continued for another 300 years until the turtles were fished out. The turtles enjoyed a brief respite during the First World War, but when export resumed, it was realized that their numbers were seriously depleted. It is reckoned that, for many years, an average of 1,600 turtles had been slaughtered each year for their keratinous scutes. The local population never consumed hawksbill meat, so most of it was discarded. Originally, the tortoiseshell was sold along with slaves, cattle, rice and copal in barter for cloth, muskets, gunpowder and items of adornment, but later the trade was for money, and while the other traded goods changed over the years, the sale of tortoiseshell remained surprisingly stable. During the Imperial era, the largest market was India, and the Malagasy merchants were Swahili and Indians.

Europe

In the seventeenth and eighteenth centuries, the Dutch had access to tortoiseshell from the East Indies and from the West Indies, as they had colonies in both areas, but little was imported from the East Indies because they concentrated on the lively trade in tortoiseshell with the Asian countries. Large amounts did come to Europe from the Dutch colonies in the West Indies, where they were mostly shipped to Amsterdam by private traders, rather than the official West India Company (Westindische Compagnie, or WIC), although taxes were still levied by the company. Dutch artisans used the beautiful material to make combs, fans, knife handles, book bindings and many small items, so there was very little waste of material, which was at the time more expensive than ivory; indeed, off-cuts were welded together to make, for example, combs (Figs. 82 and 83).

Along with the French, the Dutch were renowned for their tortoiseshell marquetry and, like the French, they produced exquisite pieces of furniture, such as cabinets with intricately designed marquetry of tortoiseshell and ivory or metals, sometimes underlying the tortoiseshell with red paint or paper to give it a red hue. This was particularly popular in the southern part of the country (Fig. 64).

Fig. 82. ▲
Black lace and tortoiseshell fan, probably for mourning, and a child's fan in blond tortoiseshell with painted insets. Probably made in England or France in the nineteenth century. Length of sticks in large fan 35cm.

Fig. 83.
Ivory box with a tortoiseshell lining and a painting of flowers under glass. European, early nineteenth century. Box diameter 6cm.

Boulle Style

It seems somewhat unfair to other skilled cabinet-makers that their furniture is described as Boulle style, after the work of the famous Frenchman, André-Charles Boulle, even when their workmanship is as masterful and when the style was not confined to Boulle's workshop alone. One such is the famous doll's house that belonged to Petronella Oortman, wife of a merchant, which is now in the Rijksmuseum in Amsterdam (Fig. 84). Doll's houses were a speciality of the Amsterdam workshops, and were exquisitely made of the finest materials. When the front doors were closed they resembled cabinets. Many rich women in Holland owned such houses, often scaled-down copies of the ones in which they lived. Petronella Oortman's was made by an unknown cabinet-maker in the early eighteenth century and was filled with expensive miniature tapestries, furniture and artworks. The case of the house stands over 1.5m tall. It is made of oak and covered with tortoiseshell and pewter marquetry, including the legs and feet, which are carved. Records at the museum say that the tortoiseshell is from loggerhead

Fig. 84. ▲
Dolls' house made in Amsterdam for Petronella Oortman in 1710. Maker unknown. The entire piece is covered in tortoiseshell and pewter marquetry. Height of the house on stand 255cm. RIJKSMUSEUM, AMSTERDAM

turtles, but this has been queried because loggerhead tortoiseshell is less easy to mould than hawksbill, and because the patterning tends not to be as attractive.

André-Charles Boulle is the first name that comes to mind in relation to French use of tortoiseshell. He was born in 1642 and made his name at a young age. By the time he was thirty, he had already been given a workshop in the Louvre galleries, an honour that was reserved for only the most favoured and skilled artists and craftsmen. He worked for many years at Versailles in the employ of Louise XIV, initially as a painter and then as an *ébéniste*, producing many different fine articles, but he is best remembered for his work combining tortoiseshell with brass or pewter. The designs were

▲ Fig. 85.
Console table from the workshop of André-Charles Boulle, made in about 1760. The marquetry is tortoiseshell and engraved brass. Height of the table 78cm.
V&A MUSEUM

▲ Fig. 86.
Top of the console table in Fig. 85, showing the intricate detail and the exquisite craftsmanship. V&A MUSEUM

often not his own but were taken from classical drawings, and the output of his workshops was prolific. He produced tables, cabinets, bureaux, armoires, pedestals, clock cases and more, using different woods and gilt-bronze mounts (Figs. 85 and 86). Boulle was not the first person to use the special combination of tortoiseshell and metals employed by him, but his work was exceptional and the style became known as 'Boulle style' – a name that persists to this day.

Of special note is the way Boulle used metal and tortoiseshell marquetry on pairs of cabinets or pedestals, using identical patterns but with the tortoiseshell as the background in one, called *premier partie*, and the brass as the background in the other, called *contre partie*, giving a positive and negative effect (*see also* Chapter 6).

Boulle had one big weakness – he could not resist buying works of art. As a result, he was always in debt, despite his great success. The problem was exacerbated when a fire swept through not only his workshop but the workshops of others as well, destroying tools and inventory, and most of Boulle's collection of artworks, including forty-eight drawings by Raphael. Boulle died in 1732, leaving large debts, which his sons, who succeeded him in the business, never managed to repay. Boulle-style furniture continued to be made in European countries well into the nineteenth century.

Possibly because of their sheer size, one of the most impressive works in Boulle style are the doors in one of the galleries at the Hermitage Museum in St Petersburg. There are four double doors, about 3m tall, entirely covered on both sides in gilded brass and tortoiseshell, with *premier partie* on one side and *contre partie* on the other.

Boulle's fame has slightly overshadowed another famous cabinet-maker by the name of Pierre Gole. He was twenty years Boulle's senior, and their work for Louis XIV overlapped for many years.

Gole was born in Holland but moved at a young age to Paris to seek his fortune. He was apprenticed to a cabinet-maker and his work subsequently came to the attention of Cardinal Mazarin, who brought Gole to the attention of Louis XIV. Gole also worked for many years at Versailles, and he is credited as being the first cabinet-maker to use floral designs in different woods and other materials on furniture. His work incorporated woods such as walnut and ebony, with tortoiseshell, ivory, pewter and gilt brass. There were always many cabinet-makers working at Versailles, but it is said that Pierre Gole was the most favoured of all (Fig. 87).

▲ Fig. 87.
Cabinet by Pierre Gole, famous for floral designs in the marquetry, here made in tortoiseshell, ivory and various woods. The cabinet was made in about 1660. Height 129cm. RIJKSMUSEUM, AMSTERDAM

Piqué Work

France was also known for the fine piqué work thought to have originated there towards the end of the seventeenth century. Piqué was a form of decoration made by inserting tiny pins, strands or small flat pieces of precious metals – sometimes together with segments of mother-of-pearl – into tortoiseshell. It was occasionally used on ivory too (*see also* Chapter 6). A typical example was the *bôite à ballon*, a small, heavily decorated box, best described as bun-shaped, which was opened by gently squeezing the sides, and very popular in France in the mid-1700s.

Piqué work was also popular in other European countries. The craft was brought by Huguenot craftsmen who fled France following the Revocation of the Treaty of Nantes in 1685. By the early eighteenth century, similar items were being made in France, Italy, England, Holland and Germany, and as few were signed, it is often not possible to tell where they originated.

The same problem can apply to furniture made in the sixteenth to eighteenth centuries, as craftsmen travelled and took their art with them. Though the style may give some indication of where an item was made – for example, furniture made in Italy often incorporated *pietra dura* – it is not always the case.

Amongst the wealthy Europeans of the eighteenth century there was a custom to send upper-class young men on a Grand Tour, visiting cities around Europe when they came of age. Souvenirs collected often included tortoiseshell boxes, sometimes with beautiful examples of tortoiseshell piqué work.

Piqué work was taken to an even more exotic level in Naples in Italy in the years around 1720–60. At that time Naples was a centre for various crafts and attracted many art connoisseurs. The work was carried out by half a dozen workshops only, and the craftsmen were known as *tartarugari* or the tortoiseshell people, the most famous of whom is probably Giuseppe Sarao. The items were made on commission, predominantly for Royal Courts and noble families, and were intended as collectors' items, not for use. A few pieces were adorned with a coat of arms.

Fig. 88.
Tortoiseshell ewer with elaborate piqué work in gold, silver and engraved mother-of-pearl. Made in Naples, probably by Giuseppe Sarao, in the mid-eighteenth century. Height 28cm (*see also* detail in Fig. 59).
GUILLAUME BENOIT

Only tortoiseshell from hawksbill turtles was suitable for the work and the objects made included boxes, candlesticks, platters, caskets and large sheets used as veneer on table-tops. Even large caskets were made of pure tortoiseshell moulded into shape with no wooden carcass to support them, and candlesticks or jug handles were formed by joining several layers of tortoiseshell and then carving it into shape. The material was filed, welded and moulded into whatever shape was required, before being inlaid with gold, engraved mother-of-pearl and, sometimes, silver in patterns of scrolls, garlands, figures or faces, all with immaculate precision (*see* Chapter 6). The production of the objects stopped suddenly and no more was made. The reason for this is unclear but is thought to be due to changes in the political scene and in fashions. Today, they are in private collections or museums (Fig. 88).

Nineteenth- and Twentieth-Century Europe

Throughout Europe, tortoiseshell continued to be used. Boxes were always popular items. Tortoiseshell was usually the main constituent but could also be used to line an ivory box; indeed, ivory and tortoiseshell were often used together (Fig. 83).

All manner of items were produced, such as page turners, fans, lorgnette frames, cane handles, writing or sewing requisites, purses, picture frames, miniature models and so forth. It was also used on musical instruments and was immensely popular for spectacle frames and hair ornaments. Many of these items were plain and unadorned, but some included piqué work. Over the years, the style had changed and the work had become much simpler and less intricate. In the mid-nineteenth century in England, there was a vogue for jewellery with piqué work. Pendant earrings, crosses, lockets and – the most popular style – round brooches were fashionable, inlaid with gold and silver, in prettily balanced designs usually incorporating flowers. Until 1885 they were made by hand, but a company in Birmingham, England, developed a method of mass production, which limited the designs, and the typical garlands of flowers gave way to more geometric outlines (Fig. 89).

The Victorians loved little trinkets, the more exotic the better, and miniature replicas of musical instruments were among collectible items. Originally delicately made, these too became popular and cruder in execution (Fig. 90).

At the less exotic end of the market were small, oblong boxes for pins, toothpicks, snuff and so forth. Many fine examples were made in tortoiseshell, but often horn was used to make the box (being thicker and a lot less expensive), with a tortoiseshell lid or a tortoiseshell-veneered horn lid (*see* Chapter 6) (Fig. 91).

Also fashionable in the early twentieth century in England were dressing-table sets. Wooden hair and cloth brushes and mirrors were covered on the back with tortoiseshell, held in place by a silver surround and with silver piqué work in the tortoiseshell. Combs were made of plain tortoiseshell with a silver spine. The sets were completed with various pots and bottles of glass, with silver and piquéd tortoiseshell lids (Fig. 92).

Tea arrived in Europe from China at the beginning of the seventeenth century and was an extremely expensive, luxury item. It was used sparingly and was stored in containers called caddies, which were originally made of porcelain. Later, wooden boxes were made that could be locked to prevent theft of the precious contents. Tea was brewed by the mistress of the house and caddies were not stored in the kitchen, so were decorative items. In the early nineteenth century, wooden caddies with tortoiseshell veneer and ivory knobs, feet, key holes and stringing became fashionable. Tea caddies are collectors' items nowadays and can fetch high prices at auction (Fig. 93).

Europeans had a fascination for exotic trinkets from far-flung lands. Two-sided combs came from Jamaica and boxes covered in tortoiseshell and overlaid with etched ivory from India. From China came snuff boxes and card cases made especially for the Western market. Many combined mother-of-pearl in geometric or floral patterns (Fig. 94). Tortoiseshell was used until the late 1900s when trade bans came into effect (Fig. 95).

Fig. 89. ▲
Two typical tortoiseshell piqué brooches and a cross pendant. The piqué work is in gold and silver. Made in England in about 1860. Length of cross 5.5cm.

Fig. 90. ▲
Collection of typical items made in England in the late nineteenth to twentieth centuries using tortoiseshell: a silver and tortoiseshell photo frame, lorgnettes, a purse, and a miniature mandolin.

Fig. 91.
Collection of horn boxes with whole or partial tortoiseshell veneer.

Fig. 92.
Dressing-table set of tortoiseshell set in silver and with silver piqué work. Made in England in 1925.

Fig. 93.
Wooden tea caddy with tortoiseshell veneer and ivory stringing, feet and finial. Made in the nineteenth century. Height 18cm.

Fig. 94.
Three card cases, probably made in China for the Western market in the late nineteenth to early twentieth century. From left: with a carved pattern; with a pressed pattern; inlaid with mother-of-pearl. Length of smallest box, 8.5cm.

◄ Fig. 95.
Modern necklace depicting a carp. Tortoiseshell, gold and pearls. Made in Scotland by Gillian O'Brien at L'Argenette Jewellery prior to the ban on the use of tortoiseshell.

Japan

Bekko Work

Without doubt, the finest tortoiseshell work produced was in in Japan, where it is called 'bekko' meaning tortoiseshell from the hawksbill turtle. It became one of the famous crafts and customs of the country, yet the custom there is little over 400 years old. Older examples of tortoiseshell can be found in the Imperial Treasure House, but these are thought to have come from China.

There is no written record of trade in tortoiseshell with either the Spanish or the Portuguese in the sixteenth century, so how and why the art of bekko started in Japan is not known. One theory is that the Portuguese introduced it, but perhaps a more logical answer is that it started when, in 1603, Japan established suzerainty over the Kingdom of Ryukyu – a string of islands to the south-west of Japan stretching towards Taiwan, and now the Kagoshima and Okinawa Prefectures. Most of Japan lies too far north to attract hawksbill turtles, which like warmer seas. With the Ryukyu islands came lots of the creatures, plus the influence of people who already used tortoiseshell, for example, for ladies' hairpins or plectra for their lute-like instruments, which were copied in Japan and became known as the Shamisen. It is still said in many countries that a tortoiseshell plectrum gives exactly the right sound to a stringed instrument due to its flexibility and softness.

In spite of having local turtles, the passion for tortoiseshell was soon so great that the Japanese were compelled to import more. In the mid-seventeenth century, their only trading partners were the Chinese and Dutch, and the latter were able to supply both the Japanese and the Chinese with turtle scutes and turtle leather as part of their trade.

There was a rapid economic growth in Japan in the mid-seventeenth century, bringing a better standard of living and more wealth, but frugality was admired and luxury forbidden. By the eighteenth century, it had become more acceptable. Further, there were restrictions covering the use of silver and gold, but not covering tortoiseshell. In the mid-twentieth century, there was again a huge increase in the country's economy, which would account for the large amount of tortoiseshell imported at that time and the ever-increasing demand for tortoiseshell items. As fashions

Fig. 96. ▲
Japanese bekko work comb. Tortoiseshell with black, gold, green and red lacquer. It was not for combing but was worn in the hair together with various pins and other adornment. Made in about 1900. V&A MUSEUM

changed, dark or blond tortoiseshell went in and out of favour, but the workmanship – which had been quite simple to begin with – became more and more complex and exquisite.

Hairpins and combs for the ladies' elaborate hairstyles never went out of fashion. They became so popular at one time that complaints were made because not only did ladies of high standing wear hairpins, but even courtesans did – and they tended to use them in abundance.

The traditional Japanese lady's costume or wedding dress would not be complete without hairpins and combs adorning the hair. Pins might be plain in colour but have intricate carving and modelling of tortoiseshell at one end, or they might have intricate lacquering and the addition of metal dust, usually with floral motifs.

The same techniques have been applied to combs, or to the little boxes that were traditionally worn by men on the *obi* or belt of their kimono, called *inro*. Writing implements, tea utensils, jewellery boxes, dishes or boxes for tobacco were all moulded or carved, inlaid with silver, gold, mother-of-pearl and other gem materials such as coral, and lacquered with the addition of metal dust to give

Fig. 97.
Japanese bekko work goldfish. Blond tortoiseshell on a mottled stand. The fish is made entirely of tortoiseshell and without a wooden carcass. Made by Ezakibekko Co. Ltd, Nagasaki.

a lighter touch. They were delicate and made to be seen as much as to be used.

The Japanese artisans have also excelled at making models of ships or carts, birds or fishes. In some instances, the tortoiseshell is moulded over a wooden base, using the mottling in the tortoiseshell to imitate an animal's spots – for example, a leopard – but done without any indication of a join in the veneer. Intricate figures are also made without a wooden core, the material moulded and carved into shape in such a way as to allow light to pass through giving a more delicate appearance (*see* Chapter 6) (Fig. 97).

Shibayama Work

Fig. 98.
Dish of ivory inlaid with mother-of-pearl, stained ivory, coral and tortoiseshell. Possibly made in the Shibayama workshops in Japan in the Meiji period. Diameter 6cm.

There was another master craftsman in Japan who incorporated tortoiseshell in his work. His name was Onogi Senzo, but he went by the name of Shibayama, taking it from the village where he was born. He is best known for his work in ivory, which he inlaid with other materials, such as coral, tortoiseshell and different colours of mother-of-pearl. Instead of inlaying materials so that the surfaces were flush and smooth, he allowed the inlays to project a little from the background, so the result was in low relief. His favourite motifs were flowers and insects. As his style of work was carried on by his sons and apprentices, it has become known generically as Shibayama work (Fig. 98).

Japan was for a long time the world's main importer and user of tortoiseshell. They joined CITES with a reservation regarding sea turtles and continued the wild-caught turtle imports for many years. Experiments with tortoiseshell from farmed green turtles were not found to be satisfactory (*see* Chapter 2).

Turtles as Food

As already mentioned, turtles and their eggs have for centuries featured in the diet of many of the local people who lived in countries where the turtles were abundant, including those who colonized the new countries; plus, they were widely used for food by sailors and discoverers. It is said that the men at the garrison on Ascension Island, where many sailing ships stopped to stock up, used to shoot the frigate birds in order to protect the turtle hatchlings, which would grow into turtles and become a valuable food source.

From the beginning of the eighteenth century, seamen attempted to take live turtles back to Europe – especially England – where they were served as a great delicacy. The turtles were kept on board on their backs with their flippers trussed, and most of them did not survive the journey. Nonetheless, the custom of eating turtle meat and turtle soup became fashionable and was considered such a delicacy that the custom continued as a sign of affluence amongst the wealthy.

The turtles that did survive the journey to London were slaughtered on arrival and served at occasions such as the annual Lord Mayor's Banquet, where it became a custom that only stopped when turtle fishing was banned. In other places, turtle feasts were served to the select few who could afford it, so became a display of wealth. Some of the silversmiths of the day even designed elaborate tureens in which to serve turtle soup, such as the spectacular solid silver tureen made in 1750 by the famous London silversmith, Paul de Lamerie. The tureen, which is almost half a metre long and weighs over 5kg, represents a green turtle lying on its back and supported by its flippers. The plastron is the cover, with a handle in the shape of a young turtle.

Eventually, ways were sought to get the fresh meat to Europe without it dying and rotting on the journey. The answer came when the process of canning food was invented at the beginning of the nineteenth century, and a large industry started up with canning factories in the coastal areas of the southern USA to can and export the products. It was almost exclusively green turtles that were slaughtered, as their meat and soup were the best quality and most tasty. The turtles were caught throughout the West Indies and Central America until the populations were decimated. By 1895, the rookeries were fished out around Florida and Texas, and turtles were brought from Nicaragua to be canned. Live turtles and turtle eggs continued to be sent to New York for slaughter there, but when refrigeration became possible, the turtles could be killed where they were caught and just their meat, calipee and calipash could be sent more economically to the rest of the USA and Europe. Subsequently, it became far less of a luxury, albeit still expensive.

Animal welfare was unheard of in those days, and the way the creatures were treated after capture was abysmal. It was easiest to catch females while they were nesting at night and 'turn' them. This involved flipping them on to their backs, which rendered them helpless. The animals were then left in the sun, sometimes for some days, until they were collected and taken to market. Those fished from the sea did not fare much better as they were dragged around by their flippers, dumped on their backs in the bottom of a boat and then piled up on a wharf – again in hot sun – to await collection.

The American company Ganday's and the English Lusty's were both famous for their green turtle soup in cans. They also sold the dried meat and cartilage for cooks to make their own soup. The English journalist Mrs Beeton's famous book, *The Book of Household Management*, first printed in the 1860s, contains a recipe for turtle soup that takes ten hours or more to prepare. Added to the dried turtle meat is beef and veal, as well as sherry. Her turtle sauce is simpler, and is to be served 'with Chicken, Calf's head, or other Brown Entrées'.

Further afield, the fashion for turtle soup had spread, and there were also canning factories in Western Australia and in Queensland, where the trade began in the mid-nineteenth century. The state governments saw turtles as a valuable resource and one to be used, as some bays were 'swarming with turtles'. Fishing continued until 1968 in Queensland and 1973 in Western Australia. Both greens and hawksbills were taken, but the numbers were relatively few compared to what the American companies were processing. Australian catches numbered a total of approximately 30,000 hawksbills and 69,000 greens over a period of eighty-four years. This may be the reason that Australia now has some of the largest colonies of turtles in the world. By the time the fishing ended, large refrigeration boats were being used to service the small boats that did the fishing, and the products were sent mainly to the United Kingdom, but also to other European countries, plus to Singapore and Japan. The desire to consume green turtles did not cease but, in 1971, the USA brought in the Endangered Species Act banning the import of turtle products. Other countries also brought in bans. It was the end of turtle soup from wild-caught greens.

Other Uses

Turtles were not only used as food or for tortoiseshell. The skin from their necks and flippers has been tanned and turned into leather, to be made into anything from wallets to boots. It resembles somewhat crocodile leather and is likewise hard-wearing.

Turtles and their eggs could be rendered down for oil, which was used by local communities for cooking or for fuel. In the late 1920s, turtle oil began to be used in cosmetics. Turtles were known for their longevity, so – if the advertisements were to be believed – using face creams made from turtle oil would rejuvenate the user. Slogans such as 'will prevent facial decline' were used to encourage people to buy face creams, soaps, cleansers and such like. The products were extremely expensive, not least because the turtle oil smelled so strongly that a lot of perfume had to be used in the products as well in order to mask the odour. They were very fashionable by 1930, but just a few years later scientists were debunking the myth because most of the products contained only a small amount of turtle oil, the rest being made up of shark oil or mineral oils, and anyhow the turtle oil had been processed to such an extent that any cosmetic benefit that there might have been was lost. The original idea for the cosmetics had come from the fact that the indigenous people of Central America had used the oil on their skins, and they had few wrinkles, but the oil they had used was unrefined. The fashion for turtle-oil based cosmetics lost favour when it was realized that it was cruel, and people switched to using plant-based products instead.

And while all this was happening, hawksbills continued to be slaughtered for their tortoiseshell (*see* Chapter 2). They were less often used for food because they have the ability to eat poisonous corals without harm to themselves, but it can turn their meat so poisonous that for humans to consume it can be lethal. Even today, there are occasional cases of people dying from eating poached hawksbill turtle meat.

In some countries, turtle eggs were believed to have aphrodisiac properties. There was no proof of that, but it is known that turtle eggs contain far more cholesterol than chicken eggs. Just as turtle oil was supposed to rejuvenate the skin, it was believed that eating turtle meat would keep a person young, a belief held because of the longevity of turtles. Turtle-based medicines were taken, especially in the Far East, to keep old age at bay.

Turtles have been used in Chinese medicine for thousands of years and, even today, the freshwater turtle farms in China are producing turtle-based medicines believed to help prevent various ailments, including dementia and age-related cardiovascular problems, though there is no scientific proof for this despite research.

Chapter 8

Other Keratins Used in the Decorative Arts

Introduction

Many keratinous materials have been used in the decorative arts. They appear as objects, carvings, inlays, veneers, jewellery and utilitarian items.

The keratin that is visible on an animal is essentially dead cells; for instance, the tortoiseshell scutes are formed in the dermis, but the hard material is no longer living. Equally, hair is produced in a follicle deep in the dermis but by the time it leaves the follicle, it is dead and being pushed out by the new hair forming and growing. For this reason it is possible, in some cases, to remove part of the keratinous material without damage to its owner; cutting hair is an example of this. In other cases, removing the keratin causes death to the animal, as would be the case with turtle scutes.

Keratinous materials are almost always coloured by the pigment melanin, which occurs in hues of creamy-white, through greys and browns to almost black.

Horn and Baleen

Horn is regarded as a natural plastic. It comes from the various members of the family Bovidae, such as cows, sheep, goats, antelope, buffalo, bison and others. Horns form as keratin sheaths over bony protuberances on the head of the animal. They should not be confused with antlers, which are a type of bone grown by the males of the Cervidae or deer family, and which are shed and regrown annually. Horns are carried by both males and females, grow throughout the life of the animal and are not shed. They come in a big variety of shapes, from the helically curved kudu horns to the straight horns of the oryx.

A horn can occasionally be lost in a fight but, apart from that, horn comes only from animals that have died. They usually grow as a single pair, though a few animals have two pairs.

Due to the wide range of animals that carry horns they vary in colour as well as shape, from the large, almost black, curved horns of the water buffalo, which are elliptical in cross-section, to the short, transversally round, pale-coloured horns of the Charolais breed of cattle. Buffalo horn is made into carvings, figures, bowls and jewellery in the Far East, mostly for the tourist trade. The horns of the Charolais were said to be the preferred horn of the French Art Nouveau jeweller, René Lalique, who favoured horn rather than tortoiseshell for his jewellery. Ox horns, which are today the most popular for making spoons, bowls, shoehorns, and such like, are gently curved and are a mixture of browns, greys, whites and black.

Horn is an extremely versatile material. Being thermoplastic, its shape can be altered more than once with the use of heat and pressure. As an example, to make spoons, a fresh horn is sliced open along its length, flattened with heat and pressure, and flat spoon blanks punched out (Fig. 99). The blanks given the required spoon shape in moulds, again with heat and pressure. Horn can also be bleached, dyed and carved, and is said to have been used by humankind since Palaeolithic times, but because it degrades after a very few centuries – largely due to insect infestation – there are no very old examples left.

Fig. 99.
Raw horn slice which has been flattened, with spoon blanks punched out.

The earliest form of drinking cup was most likely a horn. When humankind discovered that horn could be shaped and welded by heat and pressure, it opened up many possibilities. Over the centuries it has been used to make beakers, bowls, elaborate drinking horns, hunting horns, powder and snuff mills, snuff boxes, spoons, cutlery handles, combs and buttons, to name but a few items (Figs. 100 and 101). When bleached and pressed, horn was used as the panes in lanterns. In the eighteenth century, small horn boxes with intricate pictures or patterns embossed on their lids were popular; many of them portrayed a well-known figure.

When dyed, horn can be used as a simulant for other materials. Dyed black it can imitate jet and, unlike jet, it can be mass-produced and does not require hand-carving, making it a cheaper alternative. Similarly, it can be bleached and painted to resemble the more expensive tortoiseshell.

Baleen has been used in many of the same ways, plus its long, flat shape made it suitable for umbrella spokes, corset stays and scrimshaw, the last made by sailors on whaling ships between whale catches. It is difficult to tell baleen from horn when they have been treated because they lose their identifying structure.

Baleen comes in a variety of pale to dark browns but, like horn, it can be bleached or dyed. Today baleen is covered by a total ban because it is derived from whales, all of which are protected (*see also* Chapter 4).

▲ Fig. 100.
Horn snuff mull with silver lid, British, 1820.

▲ Fig. 101.
Horn box with piqué work. Probably British, made in the nineteenth or twentieth century.

Hooves

Ungulates is the name given to a large group of animals that have hooves. It includes horses, cattle, pigs, giraffes, rhinoceroses, deer and others.

Hooves grow throughout the life of the animal and are worn down by the action of walking on a hard surface. They can also be trimmed, as happens with horses when they are being shod. Hoof structure consists of tubules of keratin, forming a cylinder of hard keratin with a pad of soft keratin at the bottom.

In spite of the fact that hooves are keratin and are thermoplastic, which means that they could be moulded into different shapes by heat and pressure, they have not been much used in the decorative arts. Their somewhat awkward shape and size is possibly one reason for this. Another reason is that they have been more important in the production of animal feed, fertilizer and glue.

The most common use in the decorative arts is as small boxes with a hinged lid attached. Horses' hooves can also be found mounted with silver and containing a small glass bowl for use as an inkwell (Fig 102).

Fig. 102. ► Hoof, possibly from a deer or cattle, made into a box with a hinged lid. Height 5cm.

Hair

Hair occurs only in mammals and has very high tensile strength. It consists of tubes of pigmented, cortical cells, filled with keratin. Wool and fur are also types of hair. The shape of the hair follicle from which it grows determines whether it is straight or curly, the former being round and producing hair that is round in cross-section and straight, and the latter oval and lying at a different angle to the surface of the epidermis, and producing hair that is more oval in cross-section and curly.

Hair has been used in adornment in many parts of the world, but hair from certain species is today covered by CITES bans. An example is the extremely coarse elephant hair that comes from the end of the tail of the animal and has been used to make jewellery. It can still be found for sale in some countries. When the tail hairs are cut, they regrow, but the ban covers every part of the animal, so it is illegal to take such jewellery out of the country from where it originated.

Horsehair, from the manes and tails of horses, has also been used, and the art of weaving it still exists in some places, where it is used to make attractive small bowls or dishes. Another use is as strong upholstery fabric, especially suitable for chair seat covers, but it is notoriously scratchy to sit on.

Human hair is encountered in tribal jewellery in Africa, and in the articles of adornment worn by the peoples of the Polynesian islands. It is plaited into ropes as part of a head-dress or breast ornament, and used in conjunction with other organics such as seeds, teeth and shells.

In Europe and the USA, human hair jewellery was regarded as 'sentimental jewellery', being a physical contact to another person. In many cases, the person was deceased and the jewellery was thus mourning jewellery.

Lockets with a picture of a loved one in one side and a lock of hair in the other are the plainest form of hair in jewellery but, by the early nineteenth century, it was becoming an art form. Lockets were almost a necessity for a lady by the 1870s, but by then the hair used was no longer a simple lock but was being plaited or woven into intricate patterns or pictures and mounted in gold behind polished rock crystal or glass, often with a seed pearl surround.

Although it was customary to use the hair from one person, on occasion hair from a whole family was woven together, giving different shades in the pattern. The jewellery was fashionable enough for there to be shops and workshops specializing in it, where pieces were sometimes made from mixed human and horsehair in order to produce a larger item. Horsehair was also more coarse and easier to work, plus it was easier to obtain and usually longer.

As well as being set in metal mounts and made into pendants, brooches and rings, human hair could form the main body of the jewellery and be worked into bangles, ear-rings, ornate headdresses or watch chains. Although they looked delicate, they were quite strong. The hair had to be very long to be able to be made up; for example, a bangle needed hair at least 60cm long. Watch chains were made in sections with metal spacers in order to obtain sufficient length (Fig. 103).

The process of fashioning hair involved boiling it to make it softer and easier to work, shaping it over a mould while weaving it and boiling it again. When it cooled, it retained its newly created shape.

The art of making the pieces became a pastime for ladies, both in England and in the USA, and starter kits were available to purchase, usually supplied with the more manageable horsehair.

Fig. 103. ▲
Hairwork bracelet, made from intricately woven human hair, with metal mounts. Mid to late nineteenth century.

Porcupine Quills

There are many species of porcupine across the globe, and their quills come in different sizes and flexibility, according to the species. The African crested porcupine's quills can be about 30cm long. Quills have a structure similar to that of hair, but on a much larger scale. A few species have quills that have been used in the decorative arts.

Some porcupines are listed as endangered, while in other parts of the world the local species are numerous. Although their quills may make them look like porcupines, Australian echidnas are not related; however, their quills could be used in much the same way (Fig. 104).

To the animals, quills are a form of protection against predators. Contrary to popular belief, they cannot 'shoot' their quills when they feel threatened, but if attacked, the pointed quills can become embedded in the predator's skin.

Quills have been used on their own to make jewellery, but a more common use was to set them side by side as a covering on a wooden box, in a similar way to tortoiseshell being used as a veneer.

▲ Fig. 104.
Necklace of echidna quills. Australian, early twenty-first century.

Pangolin Scales

Pangolins are considered the most endangered of all animals. They are sometimes called scaly anteaters, although they are more closely related to bears than to anteaters. Today there are eight living species: four in Asia and four in Africa. They vary in size from 35cm to over 1m long. They are covered in small, overlapping scales of keratin, which enable them to curl up into a ball if they sense danger.

Pangolins are under threat, partly from loss of habitat but mostly from poaching. Their meat is considered a delicacy and their scales are used in Oriental medicine, where they are supposed to act as an anti-inflammatory for arthritis and to aid blood circulation, though scientific proof is totally lacking. The IUCN lists the Asian pangolins as Critically Endangered and the African ones as Vulnerable.

Their scales have, in the past, been used as jewellery, and in some places, warrior tunics were covered in overlapping scales as a form of armour (Fig. 105).

Fig. 105.
Pangolin scales on a tunic. Each scale measures about 2cm. (The size of pangolin scales varies according to the species.)

Feathers

Feathers have been used as adornment for thousands of years. As with other keratins, it is not possible to see very old examples because they disintegrate over time.

Feathers have a complicated structure. They are present in two types: those for flight and those for insulation. The former consist of a long shaft called a rachis, with lateral barbules, which interlock to give a smooth and sleek outline in order to be aerodynamic. The insulating feathers do not have interlocking barbules but are downy to give warmth.

Unique amongst the keratinous materials, feathers are not coloured by melanin but by a variety of pigments, some of which can be absorbed from their food. The colours can be very bright. Certain feathers, such as male peacock tail feathers, get their colour from light interference caused by their structure of thin, stacked sheets of transparent keratin, which reflects the light in different colours.

Feathers figure prominently in tribal head-dresses or cloaks, sometimes denoting rank by their presence or number; for example, the war bonnets worn by male leaders of the American Plains Indians. In New Zealand, Maori chiefs wore cloaks covered in kiwi feathers. In many of the Pacific Islands, especially Papua New Guinea, an abundance of brightly coloured feathers in head-dresses was used for every ceremony, to the extent that a few birds came near to extinction. In the Western world, feathers are an ever-popular addition to ladies' hats and have been used to cover or adorn dresses, and in jewellery.

In China, the use of feathers was taken further. The bright ultramarine blue feathers of the kingfisher were used as an inlay on gold or other metal plaques, and combined with pearls, jade, coral and ivory. Intricately cut and inlaid, the feathers look like vibrant blue enamel, but close inspection reveals the rachis and parallel lines of barbules of the feathers. Designs usually incorporated flowers, birds and mythical creatures, such as dragons. The items they adorned were many and varied, and included ornaments, screens and sedan chairs. For personal adornment they were added to clothes, bags, fans and fingernail guards, and made into pins and hair ornaments (Fig. 106). Many small pieces might be worn together. The workmanship was intricate and exquisite, and only ladies of a certain rank had such items, especially the head-dresses, which were the reserve of the Empress and her courtiers. It was a custom for a kingfisher feather head-dress to be used by a bride for her wedding.

Fig. 106. ▲
Pin of silver set with kingfisher feathers. Made in China for the domestic market, it would have been worn together with other pins. Length of pin 3cm.

The art of using kingfisher feathers, known as *tian-tsui*, dates back many centuries – at least as far back as the sixth century AD – and was only recently stopped.

There are 114 species of kingfisher. The Australian kookaburra is one of the largest, while the African dwarf kingfisher is the smallest at 10cm long. Not all have the beautiful blue colour on their backs and many have whitish chest feathers, while others have red or even dark colours. The most sought after blue feathers came from Cambodia, where, due to the export of large quantities to China, they were at one time the chief source of the country's income.

Avian Beaks

Bird beaks have, with one or two notable exceptions, been little used in the decorative arts. They have figured in ceremonial tribal wear, often still attached to the bird's cranium, and featured for a time in the often macabre fashions of the Victorian age. An example is the humming-bird head ear-pendants, which were made of the whole taxidermied head of the bird, complete with beak and feathers. They were not only brightly coloured, but also exotic.

Some rare birds' beaks have been mounted as jewellery; for instance, the long, slender, curved beak of the New Zealand huia or the stubbier, greenish brown beak of the cheeky parrot called a kea, have both been mounted in gold as brooches. Today the huia is extinct and the kea is endangered.

The helmeted hornbill (*Rhinoplax vigil*) has also been driven close to extinction because of the popularity of its casque – the protruding bulge at the top of its beak. A native to the Malay Peninsula, Sumatra and Borneo, and already extinct in Singapore, it is the only hornbill to have a casque large and solid enough to carve.

The casque is a pale, creamy yellow in colour with a surface colour on the top and sides of strong red, caused by the bird preening its feathers with the secretion from the preen gland, which dyes the surface of the keratin. It has been called 'hornbill ivory' due to the ivory body colour of the beak and the fact that it can be carved in much the same way as ivory, though it is a little softer. It has also been called 'golden jade'. The bird itself has been nicknamed the 'kill your mother-in-law bird' because of its raucous and maniacal cry.

The beak with its casque is made of keratin, so it is thermoplastic, which means that it can be moulded. Nevertheless the shape of the casque is normally retained and is seldom altered by anything other than cutting or carving, unless it is to bend the tip of the beak into a hook for a pendant or similar.

Helmeted hornbill casques are said to have been collected by local indigenous people for 2,000 years. They were carved and hung from a belt as ceremonial attire. In China, they have been carved since the fourteenth century and the material has remained popular, although it is now listed on CITES Appendix I. It has been made into snuff bottles, figurines, belt buckles (Fig. 107), pendants,

Fig. 107.
Belt-buckle carved from hornbill ivory, i.e. the casque of the helmeted hornbill. Note the red surface of the outside of the casque has been incorporated into the design.

beads or left simply as a decorative object, partially carved and still attached to the bird's cranium. In Japan, the casques have been made into netsuke. When worked, the red area of the casque is incorporated in the design of the object. In the case of beads, it appears as a patch of red on one side only.

Antique hornbill ivory jewellery of a Western style is occasionally encountered and may be difficult to identify. An example would be plaques of carved casque mounted in a gold surround and made into a necklace or a pendant. The tinge or red in parts of the carving aids identification.

Claws

Animal claws can denote status; for example, a necklace of grizzly bear teeth would have been evidence of a brave hunter in past times in America. As with beaks, claws could also be part of a shaman's apparel.

In countries where there were big cats, jewellery has been made incorporating the claws of lions, tigers, leopards and so forth, set in gold and sometimes combining gemstones in the design. It is less popular today because the emotional climate concerning such use of animal parts has changed.

The laws, too, have changed, and it would be difficult to sell jewellery containing big cat claws because the provenance would have to be proved. First, laboratory tests, such as mass spectrometry or DNA, would be needed to prove that the claws did not come from an endangered species. Further, the age of the claws would need to be known. Even supposing that both of those were possible, in most countries the claws would be regarded as unworked, even if they are set. Today, many organics can only be sold if they pre-date a certain time and if they have been significantly altered from their original state. Mounting claws in precious metal is not regarded as sufficient (Fig. 108).

▲ Fig. 108.
Claw brooch, probably tiger claw and made in India in the twentieth century. Length of brooch 4.5cm.

Rhinoceros Horn

There are today five extant species of rhino, all critically endangered and listed on CITES Appendix I. The African white rhino (*Ceratotherium simum*) and the African black rhino (*Diceros bicornis*) both live, as the name implies, in Africa, and have two horns. The Indian rhino (*Rhinoceros unicornis*) is found in Nepal, Bhutan and India and it has one horn. The Javan rhino (*Rhinoceros sondaicus*) is a smaller animal and, like the Indian rhino, it has a single horn, while the Sumatran rhino (*Dicerorhinus sumatrensis*) has two horns.

Rhino horn has been called compacted hair. This is incorrect as it does not grow in the same way as hair, from follicles, but from dermal papillae, which are little bumps or ridges on the skin. The horns form as tightly packed, cylindrical growths of keratin, embedded in a keratin matrix. The core of the horn is harder than the exterior due to the presence of phosphate salts.

The shape of the horns of the different species vary very slightly but they are all solid, as opposed to the keratin sheath grown over a bony protuberance by other horn-bearing animals. This allows rhino horn to be carved in high relief.

Rhino horn has been sought after in China for thousands of years. According to an old text, the first Emperor, Qin Shihuang (221–209BC), sent half a million men to open up the borders, allowing trade routes to areas from where he could obtain rhino horn and ivory, because there were so few rhinos left in China.

The horn was greatly prized and was thought to be able to detect poison. The belief was that if a poisonous liquid was poured into a rhino horn cup, it would froth. Possibly for that reason, the horn was connected to good health and longevity. It was carved and worn as plaques on belts or as jewellery, and was made into items such as boxes or paintbrush handles. It was also powdered and used in medicine, to bring down fevers.

In the thirteenth century AD, there was a large Imperial Workshop, where 150 men were employed carving rhino horn and ivory. By this stage horns were also being imported from

Africa, though the African horns were considered to be of inferior quality. The most instantly recognizable carvings are probably the intricately carved libation cups with floral decoration, in which the whole horn has been used upside-down with the wide base of the horn as the lip of the cup (Fig. 109).

In Yemen, the traditional dagger worn at the waist by men was made with a variety of materials for the handles. Not only was rhino horn considered the best, it also denoted status.

In Europe, rhino horn was also considered a valuable material and was used for a range of things, including walking canes, which were fashion items rather than mobility aids. Nowadays, the horns are much shorter than they were 200 years ago and would not be of sufficient length to make a cane. The reason for this is unknown but it may be due to genetics or to diet.

All the five species of rhino are critically endangered and are listed in CITES Appendix I. There is still a problem of poaching

Fig. 109.
Libation cup carved from rhino horn, which was believed to be an antidote to poison. Made in China in the seventeenth century. Height 10cm. V&A MUSEUM

and, although numbers have increased slightly in some areas due to patrols, they are still dwindling in others.

The horns can be cut and regrow but, because they grow quite fast, the idea that all rhinos should be dehorned to protect them from poachers is not feasible. Further, anaesthetizing a rhino is in itself dangerous for the animal.

Appendix I

Laws and Regulatory Bodies

The international agreements governing the killing of a marine turtle and the use of its parts are covered by CITES, but each country must make its own domestic laws and anyone wishing to purchase or sell an item containing tortoiseshell should first investigate the laws of their own country.

In the UK and the European Union there is a law saying that tortoiseshell may still be sold for commercial gain provided that it was worked before 1947. Further, it must be significantly altered from its original state, so a whole carapace that has only been polished is illegal, while a whole taxidermied turtle is permitted. No raw tortoiseshell can be sold. Anyone wishing to export or import an item containing tortoiseshell must have appropriate licences.

Non-signatories to CITES do not have to abide by its rules, though of course they cannot export to a member country. There are also indigenous people that have exemptions to the rules due to cultural observations. These are (in theory at least) strictly controlled.

A number of museums no longer repair their artefacts, such as tortoiseshell-inlaid furniture or clocks using tortoiseshell, while others, who have an old stockpile of scutes, believe that the furniture should be brought back to as near its original state as possible.

While the sale of antique tortoiseshell items is covered by international and domestic laws, it can be difficult to prove the age of an object and thus to know whether a sale is legal. In a case such as an English silver-mounted dressing-table set, there is a silver hallmark that indicates the date of production, but without that it is necessary to rely on known provenance or be guided by the style of the object. Tortoiseshell is less often mis-sold as antique than, for example, ivory, but the rules are flouted frankly in places such as the Far East, where in several countries tortoiseshell items are openly on sale, especially to tourists.

Most popular online auction sites have a blanket ban on selling tortoiseshell of any age, but the ban is frequently ignored and objects are listed as 'faux' tortoiseshell.

Conservation Organizations

There are several marine turtle conservation societies around the world, all doing excellent work, and many of them work together. The State of the World's Sea Turtles (SWOT) is a partnership led by the IUCN Marine Turtle Specialist Group and the Marine Species Flagship Program at the Oceanic Society. It likewise works alongside The Sea Turtle Conservation Network (WIDECAST), Sea Turtle Conservancy, and the Turtle Foundation, to name but a few. There are also many local associations and charities in the areas where turtles are found.

The largest, best-known and most influential organizations involved in turtle conservation are given here.

CITES (The Convention on International Trade in Endangered Species of Wild Fauna and Flora)

CITES is an agreement between signatories to work together to control international trade in wild animals and plants to ensure that their survival is not threatened. At the time of writing, 183 countries are signatories.

The idea for CITES was presented by IUCN already in 1963,

but it did not come into full force until 1975. Any state can join CITES by making a formal declaration to adhere to, and be bound by, the Convention. Membership is voluntary. On rare occasions a country will become a signatory but with a reservation on a certain species, meaning that they do not abide by the rules laid down for that species.

CITES' regulations cover only international trade. Each member state must make its own domestic legislation to ensure that CITES' rules can be implemented at a national level, as local problems are the responsibility of local conservation organizations and governments. Habitat loss, pollution and similar, therefore, do not come directly within its remit, though they are considered in its decisions. CITES' concern is international trade, which may pose a threat to the survival of a species.

Representatives from member states meet every three years to agree how to classify the various species. The classifications make clear the trade bans according to the degree of protection appropriate to the species. There are three levels, called appendices. Briefly, the classifications are as follows:

- Appendix I Species threatened with extinction. Appendix I provides the greatest level of protection and includes total bans on international trade in the species named, or in any part thereof. On rare occasions, exceptions can be made when the purpose of export/import is not commercial, i.e. for scientific research.
- Appendix II Species are currently not threatened with extinction but may become so, unless trade is strictly controlled. International trade can be authorized for specimens in this category but must be covered by CITES' import and export permits or a re-export certificate.
- Appendix III is the most lenient of the regulations. It covers species that are being held under observation, or for which a member country has sought help from other members in controlling trade. International trade in these species is allowed but only with the appropriate documentation and permits.

CMS (The Convention on the Conservation of Migratory Species of Wild Animals)

Being migratory animals, marine turtles are covered by a second convention, The Convention on the Conservation of Migratory Species of Wild Animals, also known as CMS or the Bonn Convention.

The agreement came into force in 1983. It is the only global, intergovernmental organization for the conservation of all forms of migratory animal: terrestrial, aquatic and avian. At the time of writing, there are 129 signatories. The goal of the organization is to protect migrating animals, wherever they are, i.e. at either destination or in transit, and to take action, 'paying special attention to migratory species the conservation status of which is unfavourable and taking individually or in cooperation appropriate and necessary steps to conserve such species and their habitat'. CMS' regulations are more flexible than those of CITES, as they are far more complicated to enact.

CMS has two appendices, briefly as follows:

- Appendix I Migratory species that are facing a very high risk of extinction in the wild and throughout all or a significant portion of their range. Members are prohibited from taking any of the animals covered and should endeavour to restore their habitats.
- Appendix II Migratory species whose conservation status is unfavourable, and need international agreements for their conservation, plus those that already have the conservation status but which would benefit from further international cooperation.

IOSEA (The Indian Ocean and South-East Asia Marine Turtle MOU)

IOSEA became effective on 1 September 2001. The MOU (Memorandum of Understanding) was concluded under CMS auspices, and signatory states held their first meeting in 2003. There are thirty-three signatories and the MOU applies to the waters and coastal States of the Indian Ocean, South-East Asia and adjacent seas, extending eastwards to the Torres Straits.

Their objectives are as follows:

> The ultimate aim of the IOSEA agreement is to maintain and recover marine turtle populations by promoting cooperation among Governments and other organizations that share this common objective. Recognizing that marine turtles have a myriad of socio-economic values, the agreement seeks to assure that any consumptive or non-consumptive use of turtles for the benefit of human beings is sustainable well into the future.

IUCN (The International Union for Conservation of Nature)

The International Union for Conservation of Nature (IUCN) is an international organization working in the field of nature conservation and sustainable use of natural resources. It was founded in France in October 1948 and is the oldest international group. Its members are organizations or institutions, and it has offices and volunteers world-wide. It is involved in data gathering and analysis, research, field projects, advocacy and education. IUCN's mission is to influence, encourage and assist societies throughout the world to conserve nature. IUCN has observer and consultative status at the United Nations, was instrumental in creating CITES, and it attends and contributes to all CITES' meetings. It is probably best known for the Red List.

IUCN Red List

The (IUCN) Red List of Threatened Species, commonly known as the (IUCN) Red List, was founded in 1964. It has headquarters in England and remains the world's most comprehensive inventory of the global conservation status of biological species. Its parent organization is the IUCN. Its website describes it thus:

> The IUCN Red List is a critical indicator of the health of the world's biodiversity. Far more than a list of species and their status, it is a powerful tool to inform and catalyse action for biodiversity conservation and policy change, critical to protecting the natural resources we need to survive. It provides information about range, population size, habitat and ecology, use and/or trade, threats, and conservation actions that will help inform necessary conservation decisions.

The status of each species on the Red List is updated every 5–10 years, and they are allocated one of nine categories: NE (not evaluated); DD (data deficient); LC (least concern); NT (near threatened); VU (vulnerable); EN (endangered); CR (critically endangered); EW (extinct in the wild); EX (extinct).

For an animal to be listed as Critically Endangered it must show a decline in population of 80 per cent or more, for three generations. For turtles, which may not mature until they are thirty-five years old, this can take 100 years.

TRAFFIC (Trade Records Analysis of Flora and Fauna in Commerce)

TRAFFIC is the wildlife trade monitoring network and works to reduce the pressure of unsustainable trade on natural biodiversity. It is a non-governmental organization, established in 1976 as an alliance of CITES and WWF (the World Wide Fund for Nature) to gather information on the trade in various threatened species, which was sorely lacking. Its headquarters are located in Cambridge, United Kingdom, and it has offices in fifteen locations of strategic importance in Africa, Asia, the Americas, Europe and Oceania.

TRAFFIC works with many other organizations, including CMS. It also works with governmental collaborations, such as the European Commission, Interpol, The World Customs Organization and many more. Its work involves constant research, publication of reports, projects, education and advocacy on the issue of wildlife trade. It has been called 'the wildlife watchdog'.

Appendix II

Quick Reference Charts for Worked Materials

MATERIAL	Tortoiseshell, mottled	Tortoiseshell, blond	Horn	Plastics
COLOUR	Honey, with dark brown patches formed of minute spots of pigment that permeate the material.	Honey.	Creams, greys, browns to almost black, sometimes in patches and following the striated structural appearance of the material.	Can replicate blond colour of tortoiseshell, but mottling appears in swirls or blobs with sharp outlines, and/or on the surface only.
TRANSLUCENCY	Translucent to almost transparent in pale areas.	Translucent to transparent.	Only translucent if very pale, bleached or in extremely thin slices.	Varies.
STRUCTURE	Little visible on highly polished material.	Little visible.	Longitudinal striations. Can look fibrous.	None visible. Air bubbles rare but possible.

MATERIAL	Tortoiseshell, mottled	Tortoiseshell, blond	Horn	Plastics
LWUV LIGHT	Chalky in pale areas. Can have a chalky 'bloom' all over, or dark areas can remain inert. Colour of fluorescence may be influenced by backing material.	Chalky.	Chalky beige in light areas. Can have overal 'bloom' of fluorescence.	Varies, but mostly inert. Casein displays chalky colour in light areas.
CROSSED POLARS	Tiny spots in rainbow of colours in pale areas.	Tiny spots in rainbow of colours.	Colours in fine stripes similar to tortoiseshell if bleached or very pale.	Swirls or patches of colour, or inert, depending on plastic. No resemblance to tortoiseshell pattern.
OTHER	Reappearance of wavy growth lines when the surface dulls with age, making it appear darker.	Can resemble plastic, but superior quality of item can suggest tortoiseshell.	Seldom takes as high a polish as tortoiseshell. May show indications of paint on surface. Often thicker than tortoiseshell would be.	Lighter in weight that tortoiseshell. Inferior quality of product can indicate plastic.

Glossary

10× magnifier A small hand-lens that magnifies at ten-power and is much used in gemmology.

Apotropaic Having the power to ward off evil.

Baldachin A canopy.

Baleen Sheets of keratinous material in the mouths of non-tooth-bearing whales, used for filtering food from water.

Barbule Part of a feather.

Bekko Tortoiseshell used by Japanese craftsmen.

Bioluminescence Light emitted by a living organism.

Black light American term for ultra-violet light.

Calipash The cartilage between the ribs in the carapace.

Calipee The cartilage between the bones in the plastron.

Carapace The hard shell on the back of a turtle or tortoise.

Carbon 14 dating An advanced laboratory test used to discover the age of an item.

Carcass The hard core of an item.

Casque A horny protuberance on the top of a bird's upper beak.

Ceilao The old Portuguese name for Sri Lanka.

Cellulose The main constituent of plant cell walls and fibres.

Ciboria A casket used in church to store the Eucharist.

CITES The Convention on International Trade in Endangered Species of Flora and Fauna. An international agreement among governments.

Collagen A structural protein in animals.

Colloid A mixture in which a substance of microscopic particles is suspended in another substance.

Crossed polars A test using two polarizing filters, which determines how a given specimen affects the light passing through.

Cross-section A section perpendicular to the axis of the item. In a turtle scute it refers to a section cut perpendicular to the surface.

Degrading process Deterioration and final collapse of a specimen.

Dermis The inner of two layers of skin.

Destructive test A test that will in some way leave a mark on a specimen.

DNA Deoxyribonucleic acid, a material that is present in nearly all living organisms and that gives genetic information.

Ébéniste French, meaning cabinet-maker.

Ectotherm A creature reliant on ambient temperature.

Electro-magnetic spectrum The entire range of electro-magnetic radiation, including X-ray and UV, IR and visible lights.

Fake An object imitating another with the objective of deception.

Family See 'Taxonomic table'.

Fluorescence Normally refers to the visible light given out when a specimen is held in X-ray, UV or some visible light (e.g. sunlight). Caused by the specimen absorbing energy in one wavelength and re-emitting it in another.

Fontanelle The gap between bones.

Foraging ground The area where an animal goes to feed.

FTIR Fourier Transform Infrared spectroscopy, a laboratory test.

Haliotis The common name given to molluscs of the family Haliotidae, including abalone, paua and ormer.

Hardness A term used in some sciences to denote how hard a material is when compared to other, known substances, which are calibrated on a scale from 1 to 10.

Hatchling A newly hatched turtle.

Head-starting A method of rearing wild-caught hatchlings till they are several months old and then releasing them.

Helical Having a spiral shape.

Herbivorous Plant eating.

Hot point test A test used to determine the relative melting point of a material, and the smell emitted.

Hygroscopic The ability to absorb and re-emit moisture.

Imbricate Overlapping, as in tiles on a roof.

Inert A lack of chemical or physical reaction.

In the round A form of carving in which the item is carved all the way round, producing a three-dimensional carving.

IUCN The International Union for Conservation of Nature. The oldest international conservation group.

Jet A special form of coal used in jewellery, especially in Victorian times.

Keratin A protein very prevalent in the animal kingdom.

Keratinous Made of, or rich in, keratin.

Lacquer Natural lacquer – a tree resin used as a coating on surfaces.

Libation cup Ceremonial cup.

Longitudinal section Section taken along the length of an item, parallel to its axis. In a turtle scute, along its length.

Lustre The amount and quality of light reflected by a specimen.

LWUV Long-wave ultra-violet light. *See* 'Ultra-violet light'.

Maki-e A form of lacquer decoration incorporating gold dust, used in Japan.

Mantilla A Spanish veil or scarf worn over a comb on the head.

Mariculture Farming or cultivation in sea-water.

Marquetry A thin layer of different woods, ivory, tortoiseshell, metals or similar that fit together to form a picture or design on the surface of, for example, furniture.

Melanin A pigment prevalent in the animal kingdom.

Melanocyte A cell producing melanin.

Midden An ancient rubbish tip.

Mohs scale The scale used to measure hardness, based on the ability of one material to scratch another one. Created in 1812 by Friedrich Mohs.

Monochromatic light A light of one wavelength only.

Mother-of-pearl The nacreous inner surface of a mollusc shell.

Natural material A material that is not man-made.

Ocean gyre Circular ocean current.

Opaque Not allowing light to pass through it.

Oracle bones Ox scapula or turtle carapaces used for divination in ancient China.

Patina The surface appearance acquired with age.

Peineta A Spanish comb used in the hair, usually to hold a veil or scarf.

Pelagic Of the open sea.

Peptide A chain of amino-acids.

Pietra dura A mosaic of different coloured stones, usually used in furniture.

Piqué A form of patterning in tortoiseshell, horn or ivory, by inlaying metals or mother-of-pearl.

Plasticizer A substance that enables another substance to become malleable.

Plastron The ventral shell of a turtle or tortoise, covering its belly.

Polariscope An instrument used for a test. *See* 'Crossed polars'

Polymer A plastic.

Protein A class of organic compounds containing nitrogen, which are an essential part of all living organisms.

Proteomics The study of proteins and their functions.

Psychopomp Creatures or spirits who guide newly deceased souls from Earth to the afterlife.

Rachis Part of a feather.

Radiocarbon *See* 'Carbon 14'.

Raman spectroscopy A laboratory test.

Reflected light Light bounced off the surface of an object.

Refractive index A measurement of the degree by which a material refracts (bends) visible light entering it from the surrounding air. A much used gemmological test for minerals.

Reliquary Box for containing relics such as pieces of bone or clothing, usually purporting to be from a saint or Holy figure.

Sargassum Genus of brown algae, also known as gulfweed.

Sclerochronology The study of physical and chemical variations in the hard tissues of (in this case) secreted keratin in turtle scutes

Scutes The horny plates on the carapace or plastron of a turtle or tortoise.

Sectility Refers to the way in which a material can be cut.

Semi-aquatic Living partly in water.

Semi-synthetic plastic A plastic consisting of part natural substances, such as milk curds, plus chemicals.

Shaman A person regarded as having access to, and influence in, the spirit world, and can practise divination and healing through going into a trance.

Simulant A material that simulates or copies a natural one, not necessarily with the intention of deception.

Skeletochronology An advanced test examining cross-sections of the bones of an animal to determine its age.

Snuff Finely ground tobacco that is inhaled without smoking.

Species *See* 'Taxonomic table'.

Specific gravity (SG) A test much used in gemmology, especially for minerals.

Stress Force applied to a material that can cause deformation.

Striated Having stripes or streaks.

Stringing The fine lines of contrasting wood or other material in the surface of a piece of furniture.

Sub-species *See* 'Taxonomic table'.

Synthetic Man-made substance or material.

Tag An identifying label attached to an animal or object.

Tartarugari Italian, meaning 'tortoiseshell people'.

Taxonomic table A table classifying living organisms. It starts with 'Kingdom' (e.g. 'animal') and subdivides through Phylum, Class, Subclass, Order, Family, Genus and Species. The genus and species are the most used and are always written in italics.

Thermoplastic Describes a material that can be altered in shape repeatedly using heat and pressure.

Thermosetting Describes a material that can be altered in shape only once using heat and pressure.

TRAFFIC The wildlife trade monitoring organization.

Translucent Permitting a little light to pass though.

Transmitted light Light that is passed through a specimen.

Ultra-violet light Light in the wavelengths beyond visible light, and which causes some materials to fluoresce. Measured in long wave and short wave (LW and SW).

UV *See* 'Ultra-violet light'.

Veneer A thin covering, usually applied to furniture to enhance its appearance.

Wavelength A measurement in the electro-magnetic spectrum.

Bibliography

Álvarez, Mari-Tere; Villaseñor Black, Charlene, 'Tortoiseshell and the edge of the empire: artistic materials and imperial politics in Spain and France'. Chapter 8, *Eighteenth Century Artworlds: Global and Local Geographies of Art* (Bloomsbury Visual Arts, 2019)

Baarsen, Reinier, *Seventeenth Century Cabinets* (Rijksmuseum Dossiers, 2000)

Beeton, Isabella, *Mrs Beeton's Household Management* (Warwick House, London, 1930s)

Bowen, Brian W, 'Tracking marine turtles with genetic markers. Voyages of the ancient mariners.' *Bioscience* (1995, Vol. 45, No. 8)

Calcagno, Robert, *Sea Turtles, the Great Odyssey* (Institut Océanographique, éditions Glénart, 2017).

Chaiklin, M, 'Imports and autarky: tortoiseshell in early modern Japan'. In K. Hofmeester & B. Grewe (eds) *Luxury in Global Perspective: Objects and Practices, 1600–2000. Studies in Comparative World History* (Cambridge University Press, 2016, pp. 218–241)

Chapman, Jan, *The Art of Rhinoceros Horn Carving in China* (Christie's Books Ltd, 1999)

Chassagneux, Agathe; Jean, Claire; *et al.* 'Unravelling behavioural patterns of foraging hawksbill and green turtles using photo-identification.' *Marine Turtle Newsletter* (no. 137, 2013)

Cooper, Diana; Battershill, Norman, *Victorian Sentimental Jewellery* (David & Charles (Publishers) Ltd, 1972)

Corbin, George A, *Native Art of North America, Africa and the South Pacific* (Harper & Row, 1988)

dei Marcovaldi, Maria AG; Santos, Armando JB; *et al.* 'Spatio-temporal variation in the incubation duration and sex ratio of hawksbill hatchlings: implication for future management.' *Journal of Thermal Biology* (2014, Vol. 44, pp. 70–77)

Deines, Tina, *Endangered Hawksbill Turtle Shell Trade is Much Bigger Than Scientists Ever Suspected* (National Geographic, 2019)

Dent, Herbert C, *Piqué, a Beautiful Minor Art* (The Connoisseur, 1923)

Dobbs, Kirsten, *Marine Turtles in the Great Barrier Reef World Heritage Area* (Great Barrier Reef Marine Park Authority, 2001)

Frazier, Jack, *Historic and Ancient Historic Interactions between Humans and Marine Turtles* (CRC Press LCC, 2003)

Frazier, Jack; Ishihara-Brito, Reiko, 'The occurrence of tortoiseshell on a pre-Hispanic Maya mosaic mask.' *Antiquity* (2012, Vol. 86, pp. 825–837)

Garnier, Julie; Hill, Nicholas; *et al.* 'Status and community-based conservation of marine turtles in the northern Querimbas Islands (Mozamnbique). *Oryx* (2012, Vol 46, Issue 03, pp. 359–367)

Halkyard, Brooke, *Exploiting Green and Hawksbill Turtles in Western Australia. A Case Study of the Commercial Marine Fishery, 1869–1973* (A HMAP Asia Project Paper, no. 160, 2009)

Hardwick, Paula, *Discovering Horn* (Lutterworth Press, 1981)

Hawkes, Lucy A; Broderick, Annette C; *et al.* 'Climate change and marine turtles.' *Endangered Species Research* (2009, Vol. 7, pp. 137–154)

Hays, Graeme C; Scott, Rebecca, *Global Patterns for Upper Ceilings on Migration Distance in Sea Turtles and Comparisons with Fish, Birds and Mammals* (Functional Ecology. British Ecological Society, 2013)

Hewavisenthi, Suhashini, 'Exploitation of marine turtles in Sri Lanka: historic background and present status.' *Marine Turtle Newsletter* (1990, Vol. 48, pp.14–19)

Hughes, George R, 'The survival situation of the hawksbill sea-turtle in Madagascar.'*Biological Conservation* (1973, Vol. 5, Issue 2, pp. 79–158)

Hughes, George R, *Between the Tides. In Search of Sea Turtles* (Jacana Media (Pty) Ltd, 2012)

Humber, Frances; Godley, Brendan J; *et al.* 'So excellent a fishe: a global view of legal marine turtle fisheries.' *Diversity and Distribution* (2015, Vol. 20, pp. 579–590)

Huxley, Roger, 'Historical overview of marine turtle exploitation, Ascension Island, South Atlantic.' *Marine Turtle Newsletter* (1999, Vol. 84, pp.7–9)

Jackson, Beverley, *Kingfisher Blue. Treasures of an Ancient Chinese Art* (Ten Speed Press, 2001)

Jaffer, Amin, *Luxury Goods from India. The Art of the Indian Cabinet-maker* (Victoria and Albert Museum, 2002)

Kjellgren, Erik; Ivory, Carols S, *Adorning the World: Art of the Marquesas Islands* (The Metropolitan Museum of Art, New York, 2005)

Kugel, Alexis, *Piqué – Gold, Tortoiseshell and Mother-of-Pearl at the Court of Naples* (Rizzoli, 2018)

Locke, Michael, *Bone, Ivory, and Horn. Identifying Natural Materials* (Schiffer Publishing Ltd, 2013)

Lunsingh Scheurleer, ThH, 'Pierre Gole, ebeniste du roi Louis XIV.' *The Burlington Magazine* (1980, June)

McCarthy, Frederick D, 'Aboriginal turtle hunters.' *The Australian Magazine* (1955, March, pp. 283–288)

McCrindle, John W, *The Commerce and Navigation of the Erythræan Sea; Being a Translation of the Periplus Maris Erythræi* (Trübner & Co., London, 1897)

McLaughlin, Raoul, *The Roman Empire and the Indian Ocean: the Ancient World Economy and the Kingdoms of Africa, Arabia and India* (Pen and Sword Maritime, 2014)

Miller, Emily A; McClenachan, Lorem; *et al. The Historical Development of Complex Global Trafficking Networks for Marine Wildlife* (Science Advances, 2019)

Milliken, Tom; Tokunaga, Hideomi, *The Japanese Sea Turtle Trade 1970–1986* (Traffic (Japan), 1987)

Morabito, Jacques; von Sauma, Johannes, *L'écaille* (Éditions Vial, 1997)

Mrosovsky, Nicholas, *Sustainable Use of Hawksbill Turtles* (Northern Territory University, Australia, 2000)

Neich, Roger; Pereira, Fuli, *Pacific Jewellery and Adornment* (David Bateman Ltd, 2004)

O'Connor, Sonia; Solazzo, Caroline; *et al. Advances in Identifying Archaeological Traces of Horn and Other Keratinous Hard Tissues* (The International Institute for Conservation of Historic and Artistic Works, 2014)

Olijdam, Eric, 'Exploitation of sea turtles in the early Dilmun period (*c*.2100–1900BC).' *Proceedings of the Seminar for Arabian Studies* (2001, Vol. 31)

Pearson, Ryan M; van der Merwe, Jason P., *Distinguishing Between Sea Turtle Foraging Areas Using Stable Isotopes from Commercial Barnacle Shells* (Nature Research, Scientific Reports, 2019)

Pilcher, Nicholas J; Perry, Lisa; *et al.* 'Short-term behavioural responses to thermal stress by hawksbill turtles in the Arabian region.' *Journal of Experimental Marine Biology and Ecology* (2014, Vol. 457: 190–198)

Quye, Anita; Williamson, Colin (eds), *Plastics, Collecting and Conserving* (NMS Publishing Ltd, 1999)

Remetter, Ruth, *Schildpatt, das material und möglichkeiten seiner verarbeitung* (Munich, online publication, 2002)

Ricketts, Howard, *Objects of Vertu* (Barrie & Jenkins Ltd, 1971)

Rieser, Alison, *The Case of the Green Turtle* (John Hopkins University Press, 2012)

Rijkelijkhuizen, Marloes, *Tortoiseshell in the 17th and 18th Century Dutch Republic* (Archeopress, 2010)

Ross, James Perran, *Hawksbill Turtle Ranching and Captive Breeding* (CITES, 2018)

Schaverien, Adele, *Horn, Its History and Its Uses* (Everbest Printing Co. Ltd, 2006)

Segura, Luciano N; Cajade, Rodrigo, 'The effects of sand temperature on pre-emergent green sea turtle hatchlings.' *Herpetological Conservation and Biology* (2010, Vol. 5, pp. 196–206)

Slater, Richard, 'Tortoiseshell piqué jewellery.' *Antique Collecting* (The Antique Collectors' Club, Dec. 1998/Jan. 1999, pp. 34–35)

Snover, Melissa L; Balasz, George H; *et al.* 'Age and Growth Rates of Hawaiian Hawksbill Turtles (*Eretmochelys imricata*) using Skeletochronology' *Marine Biology* (2013, Vol. 160, no. 1, pp. 37–46)

Solomon, SE; Hendrickson, JR, 'The structure of the carapace and plastron of juvenile turtles, *Chelonia mydas* (the green turtle) and *Caretta caretta* (the loggerhead turtle).' *Journal of Anatomy* (1986, Vol. 145, pp. 123–131)

Soulat, Jean, 'L'artisanat de l'écaille de tortue marine sur la site de la Cour Napoléon, Grand Louvre, Paris (1e arrondissement) aux XVIIe – XVIIIe siécles: témoin de l'exotismedes Petites Antille.' *RAIF* (2016, Vol. 9, pp. 299–321)

Spotila, James R, *Sea Turtles. A Complete Guide to their Biology, Behaviour and Conservation* (The John Hopkins University Press, 2004)

Van Houtan, Kyle S; Andrews, Allan H; *et al. Time in Tortoiseshell: a Bomb Radiocarbon-Validated Chronology on Sea Turtle Scutes* (The Royal Society Publishing, 2016)

Velador Newsletter, 'The tortoiseshell trade.' *Sea Turtle Conservancy* (2007, Issue 3)

Watt, George, *Indian Art at Delhi 1903* (Motilal Banarsidass, Delhi, 1903)

Weber, Sam B; Weber, Nicola; *et al. Ascension Island as a Mis-Atlantic Development Habitat for Juvenile Hawksbill Turtles* (Marine Biological Association of the United Kingdom, 2014)

Wilk, Christopher (ed.), *Western Furniture, 1350 to the Present Day* (Philip Wilson Publishers/V&A, 1996)

Wilmé, Lucienne; Waeber Patrick O; *et al. Marine Turtles Used to Assist Austronesian Sailors Reaching New Islands* (Elsevier Masson SAS, 2015)

Woodrom Rudrud, Regina, 'Forbidden sea turtles: traditional laws pertaining to sea turtle consumption in Polynesia (including Polynesian outliers).' *Conservation & Society* (2010, Vol 8, Issue 1, pp. 84–97)

Wyneken, J, *The Anatomy of Sea Turtles* (U.S. Department of Commerce NOAA, Technical Memorandum. 2001, NMFS-SEFSC-470, 1-172)

Züber, Hüsnü, *The Ottoman Spoons* (The Turkish Journal of Collectable Art, October 1985, Issue 7)

Index